ONCE UPON A
CAMPUS

ONCE UPON A CAMPUS

Lessons for Improving Quality and Productivity in Higher Education

by
Daniel Seymour

AMERICAN COUNCIL ON EDUCATION ★
ORYX PRESS ★
Series on Higher Education
1995

10 9 8 7 6 5 4

The rare Arabian Oryx is believed to have inspir.   myth of the unicorn. This desert antelope became virtually extinct in the early 1960s. At that time several groups of international conservationists arranged to have 9 animals sent to the Phoenix Zoo to be the nucleus of a captive breeding herd. Today the Oryx population is over 1,000, and over 500 have been returned to the Middle East.

Published by The Oryx Press, an imprint of Greenwood Publishing Group, Inc.
88 Post Road West, Westport, CT 06881
www.oryxpress.com

Published simultaneously in Canada
Printed and Bound in the United States of America

⨂ The paper used in this publication meets the minimum requirements of American National Standard for Information Science—Permanence of Paper for Printed Library Materials, ANSI Z39.48, 1984.

Library of Congress Cataloging-in-Publication Data

Seymour, Daniel, 1947–
    Once upon a campus : lessons for improving quality and productivity in higher education / by Daniel Seymour.
    p. cm. — (American Council on Education/Oryx Press series on higher education)
    Includes bibliographical references and index.
    ISBN 0-89774-965-0 (alk. paper)
    1. Education, Higher—United States—Administration. 2. Total quality management—United States. I. Title. II. Series.
LB2341.S447 1995
378.1'07—dc20   94-47394
                                                                      CIP

P

To Raymond, my dad.

CONTENTS

PREFACE

A Washington, D.C. newspaper columnist suggested recently that the political Left's ability to mobilize a mass movement in this country had withered. Today, he said, civil rights groups, consumer organizations, and organized labor function more as Washington pressure groups than as true conduits to the grass roots. They've become more adept at finessing the regulatory process and filing lawsuits than reaching a broad public audience. To nail down his point, the columnist then quoted a senior White House official, "What's happened to these interest groups is what happened to academics: They started to speak only to themselves."

It is easy to dismiss the cynical words of a Beltway politician. Indeed, we would be well advised to do so more often. But, in this case, there may be more than a speck of truth embedded in the remark. Confirmation comes from an august group of higher education and industry leaders who, in the fall of 1993, issued a 160-page report entitled *An American Imperative: Higher Expectations for Higher Education*. The group, formally known as the Wingspread Group on Higher Education, began its open letter to "those concerned with the American future" in this way: "A disturbing and dangerous mismatch exists between what American society needs of higher education and what it is receiving."

The remaining 159 pages do nothing to reduce the angst described in the group's first few words. Time after time, in page after page, more than 30 essay writers—college presidents, journalists, consultants, and industrialists—passionately describe variations on this opening theme: the unresponsive nature of our colleges and universities.

We aren't listening. We are too busy talking. And we are too busy talking to each other. Society and all of its individual stakeholders (students, industry, parents, and politicians) want value in education. Students want better teachers, ones who will stimulate them in the classroom and help them succeed. They want a course of study that is coherent and comprehensive and will give them a foundation on which to build careers and improve the quality of their lives. Industry leaders realize that in a global economy they need graduates who have an array of competencies, including technical, teamwork, communication, and leadership skills. Most of all, industry needs people who have been imbued with a love of learning. Those who write the tuition checks (parents, as well as students through part-time jobs and industry through tuition reimbursement programs) and those who fund the budgets (local, state, and federal governments) want all that as well, plus a solid return on their investment.

These stakeholders expect the same thing in a college education that they expect in a toaster oven or a new home—utility. Skip the rhetoric. Forget about the cute accessories or the quaint features. People want to be assured that what they purchase today will be useful tomorrow. They work hard for their money, and so when they spend it, on anything, they want good quality at a fair price.

We aren't listening.

PURPOSE

The purpose of this book is to address directly, forcefully, and prescriptively the issue of improving performance in higher education, not just from the perspectives of a college professor or administrator but also from the perspectives of a wide array of stakeholders. The intent is to extend the discussion we have been having with ourselves over the issues of quality and productivity to a broader audience. A more inclusive approach seeks solutions to our problems in such widely disparate fields as systems theory, operations research, quality management, fluid dynamics, human resource management, and organizational development.

The chasm between what we do in higher education and what society needs must be bridged. But it is a mistake to think that new wine will come from old bottles. The answers to budgetary problems and calls for accountability will not be found in more early retirement programs or reformulated accreditation guidelines. We won't be able to respond to higher expectations through such timeworn mechanisms as program review and tenure systems. Our tradition-bound threats to state legislators ("If we don't get the money we'll have to limit enrollment," "We are losing our best professors to other higher-paying institutions") have a cry-wolf air about them.

We can't buy, tax, talk, or cut our way out of this one. We must change. And new, fresh ideas, from different perspectives and unique angles, are our best hope for doing so.

The stakes are high, the incentives strong. Indeed, if we don't assume the role of bridge builders—if we don't start speaking and listening to people other than ourselves and pursuing breakthrough ways of thinking and acting—the legislators and agency bureaucrats will necessarily make a bad attempt to bridge the gap between "what society needs and what it is receiving" for us.

ARRANGEMENT

The arrangement of this book suggests that comprehensive performance improvement is a matter of design, not circumstance. The book's five-part framework includes

- direction setting,
- process design and management,
- feedback,

- enablers, and
- personal involvement.

These framework structures, which are detailed in this book's introduction, serve as an organizing scheme for a series of stories, each of which is based upon a real event that was shared with me by a campus practitioner. The storytelling format has two advantages: stories strike an emotional chord and they offer a vivid representation of a concept that fosters learning. The lessons that emerge from the stories and the detailed explanations that follow provide a rich description of 14 key areas that dramatically affect the quality and productivity of our colleges and universities. In order to tie the stories, lessons, and explanations back into individual experience, each lesson concludes with a set of questions intended to stimulate readers to reflect on their own professional work and institutional situation.

The framework and lessons do not fit the basic criteria of a valid categorization system: they are not mutually exclusive and totally exhaustive. The lessons overlap and may sometimes seem redundant. I apologize. The work of performance improvement is messy business. Nonetheless, I am of the opinion that the framework and lessons I have chosen to describe are both critical to higher education and largely unexplored in any systematic fashion.

It is also important to note that the book can be used in two distinct ways. One is as an audit tool. To use the book in this way, pay particular attention to the story that introduces each lesson. If the story resonates with you on a personal level—"Boy, that kind of thing happens here all the time"—then you should study the accompanying explanation and reflect on the end-of-lesson questions. In this manner, the lessons act as a checklist that can help you redirect institutional resources or individual energies to specific areas.

The book can also be used as a planning tool. This approach involves a less emotional and more mechanistic pass through the material. Assume that each lesson will be of equal value to you and study the performance improvement framework described in the introduction. Taken together, the framework and the lessons provide a comprehensive and systematic way to think about improving quality and productivity at your institution.

As an audit tool or as a planning tool, I believe the book offers a practical methodology for adding value to our educational enterprises.

ACKNOWLEDGMENTS

I have many people to thank. I have had the privilege of visiting numerous college campuses in the last several years. Without fail, the people I have talked to and worked with have been generous with their time and their willingness to share what they have learned. If there is any wisdom in this book, it is because of their hard-won insights. The good people at Oryx Press have made the task of writing and publishing this book less painful than expected. At the head of the line of pain reducers are Kristan Martina and Susan Slesinger. Most important, I have been blessed with wonderful and talented friends who have the courage and grace to tell me when I am wrong and what I might do to fix things. Due to the efforts of Maury Cotter, Monica Manning, and Deborah Teeter, this book is decidedly better than it was.

And to my personal physician—Matilde Parente—*mille grazie, bella.*

INTRODUCTION

Few things are more frustrating than having a good idea fail. You think, "Surely they will see the value in this and get excited about it, as I am," but it doesn't happen that way. The nagging question you ask yourself is *why*. After all, it really was a good idea. There are two answers: either too few people wanted the idea to succeed or too few people knew how to make it succeed.

There are multiple variations on the first possibility. Everyone has witnessed the manager or supervisor who responds to a new idea with, "That'll never work here." An idea can also be greeted with the kind of ho-hum enthusiasm that sends a subtle message, "Thanks, but no thanks." For whatever reason (they are too close to retirement; they built the old system), these people are not committed to seeing you or your idea succeed. Another idea-busting scenario is when the people who do the work—secretaries, clerks, analysts—are not consulted about the idea, so they feel no ownership or involvement in the change process. Because they have no stake in the idea's success, they have no qualms about its failure. Perhaps the most frustrating scenario is when the rhetoric is there—"Great idea, Dan, really. We need to do something like this"—but nothing happens. The idea, thirsty for water and care, dies a quiet death.

All of these instances result in a self-fulfilling prophecy. No one needs or wants the idea to succeed, so it doesn't. The organization identifies the new idea as a foreign object, something to be attacked, neutralized, and expelled. It means change, and change usually evokes a potent immune response.

The other answer to the *why* question is that although some people may *want* an idea to succeed, they do not necessarily know *how* to make it succeed. In this case, the failure is not a matter of intransigence or willful neglect but one of capability. The simplest ideas have an unsettling effect on a stable system because change is not an event; it is a series of events. Generating a new idea is the easy part. You know there is a need and your idea will work. But others, although they may be willing to entertain the notion that, indeed, there may be a better way, do not see the situation through your eyes. To you, the idea appears clear and sharp. Others squint. To them, your idea has fuzzy edges and vague connections.

Failure under such circumstances is the result of poor conceptualization. The people involved are not working from the same blueprint. Each has a different understanding of the idea's core meanings and fundamental relationships. Like the blind men touching different parts of an elephant, every individual thinks and acts differently based upon his or her unique interpretation of the idea. In effect, there is no common, agreed-upon understanding of either the elephant or the idea. The result tends to be pockets of success and uneven activity, not the comprehensive change initially envisioned.

Improving the performance of a college or university is a good idea. Who would disagree with the concept of more and better student learning? Research and scholarship are integral parts of many institutions' missions as well. Would anyone argue against improving the quality of scientific inquiry? We also talk about service in higher education. Is anyone against our becoming a more capable community partner? In all aspects of our venerated three-legged stool—teaching, research, and service—we should be pursuing increasingly efficient and effective ways of conducting our work. Improvement is a good idea, yet few beyond the campus walls would agree that we have made the idea of performance improvement a priority, let alone a reality.

We cannot show that the chart-topping tuition increases of the past decade have been matched by breakthrough increases in the rate of student learning. There is little evidence to suggest that those same tuition increases have been accompanied by a dramatic upswing in recruiter satisfaction, that we are doing a much better job of graduating students with the kind of competencies industry needs to remain competitive. How about our service commitment? Would most community members agree that the last 10 years have produced a surge of active partnering efforts on the part of their local colleges and universities?

Improving performance is a good idea, but most institutions of higher education would be hard-pressed to show strong trend lines on any quality or productivity indicators that their stakeholders value. Colleges and universities can check off the number of academic programs they have or point to the increased percentage of their faculty with Ph.D. degrees. They can brag about a successful capital campaign, a new electron microscope, or the number of volumes in the library. They get very, very quiet, however, when asked to explain the methodology being used to improve teaching and learning. The silence is palpable when colleges and universities are asked to demonstrate the ways in which they are becoming more productive (other than the anachronistic student-faculty ratio).

Why? The answer is the same one offered earlier: either too few people really care about improving performance or too few people know how to make it happen. There is no doubt that new ideas, especially those that come from outside the academy, often face a cold reception on a college campus. Our institutions value conservation. Their decentralized organizational structures are extraordinarily well designed to weather even the most turbulent storms of change. Personnel policies such as tenure and norms such as "academic freedom" function as crossbeams on the structure of higher education, lending additional support to the existing enterprise. Indeed, the ability of universities to withstand the rise and fall of governments, as well as countless wars and social movements, is the stuff of mythology.

For want of a critical mass of change agents, the adoption of new ways to increase the quality and productivity of educational services is often unsuccessful. But the tendency to embrace the status quo, however highly evolved in the culture of higher education, is only part of the difficulty. Our seeming inability to add ever-increasing amounts of value to our educational services and research endeavors is not simply the result of new ideas butting heads with old ways. The problem is more complex than the stereotype of entrenched academics or the evils of tenure. Instead, the problem turns on the inability of educational leaders and a core group of willing followers to conceptualize the issue of performance improvement properly.

Ask professors about performance improvement and they will tell you about a course they are currently revising or a conference they recently attended. Ask deans and you are likely to hear about a new major being offered. Ask presidents and the conversation may switch to the change in graduation (or persistence) rates. All of these are valid interpretations of performance improvement, or valid interpretations of an elephant. The problem comes when you attempt to enhance systematically the performance of an institution and its programs by relying on these disjointed notions of improvement.

The idea fails because there is no way to align or integrate these disparate views. Each person conceptualizes improvement differently. Each operates according to his or her own theory of the whole, based upon his or her experience with a particular part. Even if people were willing to act in the best interest of the institution first and their individual or territorial self-interest second, they do not know how. They are trying to sing in harmony, but each person is reading from a different page of sheet music. To the outside world, to the world beyond the campus walls, the result is noise, not music—a cacophony, not a symphony.

The proposed performance improvement framework is designed to help an institution and its members think more clearly and uniformly about improving quality and productivity. The framework proffers an answer to the brainteaser "How can we do more with less and do it better?" It is a same-page symphony.

There are five components:

1. Direction setting
2. Process design and management
3. Feedback
4. Enablers
5. Personal involvement

The Performance Improvement Framework Chart, on page xx, shows the relationships among the five components. Numbers in boxes indicate the relevant lesson numbers in this book.

The first three components act as a tightly linked system—in effect, an organizational learning cycle. The framework begins with direction setting. In prehistoric times our forebears wandered the earth aimlessly. Getting from one spot to another was an exercise in guesswork. Later, our traveling became more efficient and effective because of our ability to employ celestial navigation—the North Star. In the last few centuries our performance improved still more because of the compass, a device that uses the earth's magnetic fields to help us align our movements with true north. Sailing a ship across the Pacific is no different from organizing a college or university for performance improvement. In both instances, it is immensely helpful if we can come to some agreement on which way to aim the pointy end.

The second component is process design and management. In an organization, processes are the vehicle through which work gets produced. A college or university has many such processes: course scheduling, advising, grant writing, contract administration, and so on. The institution is only as good as its processes, and *goodness* can be defined as the ability of the institution to meet its stated aim, its true north. To that end, processes need to be purposefully designed and willfully managed. They need to be planned as logical, streamlined pathways and directed so that institutional resources—capital and people—are used to maximum effectiveness. Quality, in this light, is not a fortuitous event (being included in *U.S. News and World Report*'s list of best colleges or having one of your professors win a Nobel Prize) or an exercise in wishful thinking (declaring oneself to be excellent or developing a catchy advertising campaign); it is the expected result of a conscious improvement strategy.

PERFORMANCE IMPROVEMENT FRAMEWORK

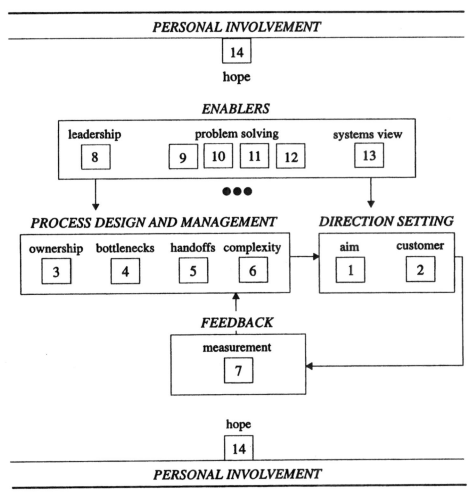

Feedback is the third component in the framework and the key variable in the learning cycle. Direction setting establishes an aim, and process design and management provides a rational system for sailing the enterprise. The link between direction setting and process design and management is a feedback loop that measures where you are versus where you want to be. An analysis of the resulting gap produces the information used to alter management practices or purposefully redesign processes. Without the ability to assess performance and learn from that assessment, the circuit is incomplete. It is as if the bridge of a vessel, its engine room, and its navigational system were unable to communicate with one another. Without measurement and feedback, the enterprise is either on automatic pilot or adrift. Nautical history suggests that either circumstance can lead to disaster, expecially in stormy seas.

These three components must work together if the quality and productivity of the institution are to improve. An awe-inspiring aim supported by a weak process component will leave individuals feeling betrayed as dreams clash with reality. A process, beautifully designed and artfully managed, can degrade over a relatively short period of time if process managers do not generate solid performance measures and feedback loops. In contrast, when all three components work together the organization becomes increasingly skilled at creating, acquiring, and transferring knowledge, and at modifying its behavior to reflect new insights. The result is an organization that learns.

The framework also describes an enabling component that helps the institution develop, implement, and improve the learning cycle. The enablers function as a catalyst. In a chemical reaction, a catalyst is a substance that facilitates or speeds up a reaction while remaining unchanged itself. In the improvement scheme, enablers are not explicitly involved in the learning cycle defined by the linking of direction setting and process design and management via the feedback loop. Still, these enablers, such as leadership and problem-solving approaches, have a critical influence on the rate at which the organization creates the knowledge required to alter its practices.

The final component is personal involvement—the degree to which individuals exercise control over their own work environment. Personal involvement brackets the framework because the sharing of power—information, ideas, resources—greatly influences the ability of the organization to learn and adapt. For example, broad-based personal involvement in direction setting yields a shared vision that both inspires and informs daily actions. Without such involvement, direction setting is usually reduced to an administratively derived statement at the front of an accreditation report. Feedback is also enhanced by personal involvement. When individuals are involved in the process of identifying performance measures, feedback is perceived as a useful way to guide future action; when the measures are imposed, feedback is seen as one more whack being delivered by the stick of a command and control bureaucracy. Involvement facilitates improvement. Unlike an enabler, however, which aids learning while remaining unchanged itself, increased levels of personal involvement yield leaps in performance, which in turn lead to greater personal involvement in the institution.

As we have noted, improving the performance of a college or university is a good idea, especially now, when our institutions are under tremendous pressure to contain costs and deliver more and better educational services. Within the context of the proposed framework and its components, this book prescribes a series of lessons to help make continuous improvement both an institutional strategy and a personal imperative. There are 14 lessons in all: four in process design and management, one in feedback, six in the enablers component, one in personal involvement, and two in the first component, direction setting—to which we now turn.

PART 1

DIRECTION SETTING

PERFORMANCE IMPROVEMENT FRAMEWORK

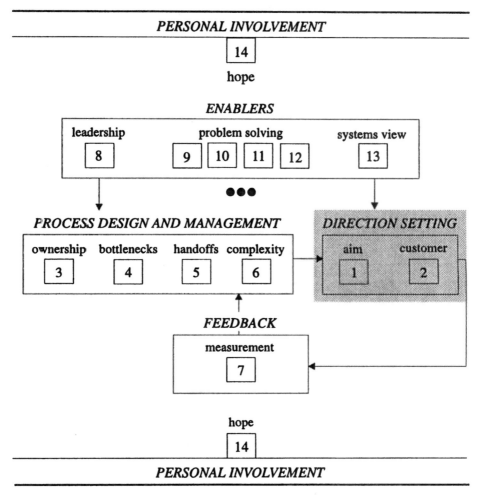

PERSONAL INVOLVEMENT

14

hope

ENABLERS

leadership   problem solving   systems view

8   9 10 11 12   13

●●●

PROCESS DESIGN AND MANAGEMENT   *DIRECTION SETTING*

ownership bottlenecks handoffs complexity   aim   customer

3   4   5   6   1   2

FEEDBACK

measurement

7

hope

14

PERSONAL INVOLVEMENT

LESSON 1

"Begin with the end in mind."

Roger worked at the end of a line that made display monitors for computers. His job was to do final assembly and to inspect. Each day, about 50 display monitors came to Roger. He knew his job well. He carefully inspected and tested each monitor to make sure it met acceptable specifications. Any monitor that didn't meet standards, he rejected. Those that were exceptional, he marked "special," and they were used on demonstration models.

Roger knew his job was important. He knew that customers expected quality and that a computer wouldn't be a quality computer if the display monitor didn't work. The specifications were necessary to ensure display monitors worked. He knew that about 16 percent of the monitors didn't meet specifications and about 10 percent were exceptional. His supervisor used these figures as a benchmark to make sure that Roger was doing his job well. Not too many, not too few. Roger was confident he was doing quality work for the company and its customers.

Roger never actually saw the completed computers. He never saw how the display monitors worked in the end. He wasn't sure how they were assembled into the computer, and he never saw a customer use one. He also never saw the steps Michele, Teresa, and Laura went through to assemble the three major components of the monitor before he got them, so he didn't know what caused the monitors to have different brightness levels or unequal resolution.

Then one day a new supervisor, Rose, came to the company. She said, "What if all display monitors met specifications?" Roger laughed. New supervisor. She didn't understand that if he passed all the monitors some of the computers wouldn't work properly, customers would be mad, and they would be reluctant to buy the company's computers in the future.

"No," Rose explained. "We won't change the specifications. We'll improve the process so that all monitors meet specifications." Roger couldn't do anything about that. The monitors were nearly done when they came to him. She explained that they would have to study the whole process of making display monitors, from design through completion, step by step.

So Roger, Michele, Teresa, Laura, and Rose got together and worked on the whole process. They found out what steps in the process resulted in variation. They made improvements and reduced the number of rejected display monitors to 2 percent. Then they went back to work. This time they raised specifications. The new aim was to make all display monitors exceptional.

A new aim. A new paradigm. A new computer company.

❖

Matty was a college professor. She taught Rural Sociology 417 to third- and fourth-year students. Every year about 90 students came through on her conveyor belt. Her job was to add knowledge and test kids to make sure they met minimum standards. Any student below the minimum did not graduate. Any student who excelled was labeled "exceptional" and given honors.

Matty knew her job well. She knew that society and those who hired graduates expected them to have a minimum standard of knowledge. Tests and grades were a way to ensure that students met the standard. She knew that in any given year about 16 percent of the students at her university didn't make it and about 10 percent graduated with honors. These were benchmark figures to evaluate how well she was doing. Not too lenient, not too tough.

Matty was confident she was doing her job to provide for an educated society. She never saw what happened to the students after her classes—whether they graduated, got a job, or did well in their jobs. She didn't know whether or how they used the knowledge from RS 417 in their lives, their next courses, or their work. And she never saw the steps the students went through before they got to her, at home, in elementary and high schools, and in their other college courses. She didn't see what contributed to each student's different level of understanding and strengths.

Then, one day, a new dean came. He said, "What if all students were successful?" Matty laughed. To think that some of these students would be rated "successful" was an insult to education. They didn't comprehend the material or complete the assignments, and they certainly didn't understand rural sociology.

"No," he explained. "We won't change the expectations. We'll change the process so that all students can meet the expectations." Matty couldn't do anything about that. Too much happened earlier over which she had no control. Too much happened later about which she had no knowledge.

But suppose, just suppose, that we could get together and develop a process that would result in all students meeting high expectations? Even graduating with honors? Imagine university spokespersons bragging about the achievements of seniors and the quality of the graduating class instead of the SAT scores of entering first-year students. Suppose that every year students would learn and do more than the class that preceded them.

*A new aim: to look at education as a process and identify
what contributes to the overall success of each student.
Aiming at success for each person. No one fails. No student
is scrapped.*

*A new aim. A new education system. If we can do it for
computers, why not for students?*[1]

❖❖❖

Visions, missions, goals, aims. Some people use these terms inter-
changeably; others spend a great deal of time and effort making fine
distinctions. I choose the middle path. A vision is the answer to the
question "What do we want to create?" A mission, or purpose, is the
answer to another question, "Why do we exist?" Goals state *what* is to
be achieved and *when*—say, a 20 percent increase in retention rates in
two years. An aim, in my mind, is a hybrid. It's largely vision, with a
hint of mission and a healthy splash of goal setting. Placing a man on
the moon before 1970, that was a powerful aim.

The "vision thing," however you wish to define it, has been a very
popular organizational pastime in recent years. Most people involved
in "visioning" are well intentioned. I believe they understand the value
in knowing what they are trying to create. In spite of good intentions,
however, most of the time and energy devoted to developing visions,
missions, and goals is of little real value. Visioning has become an expectation; we do it because people expect us to do it. New presidents
are expected to describe in inspiring prose their vision for tomorrow.
Strategic planning exercises have become treks to off-site retreats where,
after some discussion, debate, and a pleasant lunch, key executives
revisit their vision and hammer out a set of operating goals for the
upcoming year. The resulting document is copied, bound, and put on
a shelf—right next to its predecessor.

The result is that most answers to the question "What do we want to
create?" are top-down, platitudinous litanies that have little or nothing
to do with the day-to-day work in the organization, which is a tragedy.
(See also lesson 8, "Followers, not leaders, are the best judges of hy-

pocrisy)". A clear vision, a carefully crafted aim, is uplifting; it inspires commitment, fosters risk taking, and generates purposeful action. And, most significant, it keeps us centered on what is truly important.

Moreover, there is a distinction between doing things right and doing the right things. The former is hard work and careful execution, but the latter determines whether such diligence will produce the best possible outcome. When we lose track of the aim, good intentions and dedicated effort are often wasted. Losing sight of the aim is an everyday problem in our institutions and our society.

Over the last several years, for example, our society has become fixated on crime. Politicians, responding to citizens' fears and media coverage, have enacted increasingly strict sentencing guidelines and allocated larger and larger proportions of flat or decreasing budgets to "corrections." Crime is a growth industry: more judges, more prosecutors, more police . . . and a whole lot more jails. Everyone is working hard on the problem. The police, the lawyers, the construction workers, and the corrections officers are doing things right.

But are they doing the right thing? In the frenzy to do something, have we lost sight of the aim? The aim, it would seem, is a society in which people respect each other's rights and properties. Such a society would have few jails, because there would be little need for them. So, if the aim is a society with few jails, how do we get there by spending all of our time, energy, and money on a system that requires more jails? We have lost our way.

Another example. In recent years there has been considerable debate in higher education over grade inflation: studies have been conducted, articles written, and a slew of impassioned letters-to-the-editor published. Some of the analyses are quite rigorous. The arguments are both forceful and fervent, suggesting that the diminution of tough standards has led to the devaluation of a college degree and a lessening of quality. Stanford University recently garnered national headlines when, after a comprehensive study of grading practices, it decided to restore the no-pass (NP) grade and restrict a liberal add-drop policy. The driving force behind the new regulations was the belief, by many Stanford professors, that the system was too lenient and too bloated with A's and B's. As the head of the faculty committee that developed the new policy noted, "This sends a clear message to the students that we take the life of the mind seriously."[2]

But, again, what is the aim? If the aim is to rank and sort students, then grade inflation is definitely a problem; it lessens our ability to discriminate between levels of goodness. If the aim, however, is student success, then the only legitimate purpose of an examination or a grade is to enable the teacher and student to work together to decide what to do next. In such an environment, A's and B's don't reflect a weak-kneed approach to education but, rather, an indication that real learning is taking place, that the student—regardless of how many times he or she had to drop and retake the course—has indeed mastered the material. With an aim of student success, not ranking and sorting, firmly fixed in the minds of students, professors, and administrators, the grade takes on a unique meaning. It is an assessment of the amount of learning that has taken place, which is used, in turn, to inform further improvement efforts, not a means to derive artificial thresholds to determine who gets into graduate school.

Without an aim, we wander. We lose sight of what is important. Our decisions are reactive, and we spend inordinate amounts of time and scarce resources on insignificant issues or wrongheaded ideas, like debating the evils of grade inflation (when student success is what is important) or building jails at breakneck pace (when developing educated, employable, and respectful citizens is the ounce of prevention we so desperately need).

W. Edwards Deming, the late quality expert, described the issue in terms of the problems of today versus the problems of tomorrow.[3] He suggested that it is easy to stay bound up in the tangled knot of the problems of today, becoming ever more efficient in solving them. By narrowly focusing on doing things right, we miss the chance to forge a constancy of purpose that ties means to an end, the chance to do the right things right. Getting tough on crime and combating grade inflation are not aims; creating a society of individuals who value each other, creating a school that is obsessed with student learning—now, those are aims worthy of a passionate commitment.

Without such aims, there is no shared understanding of what is truly important. Activities become disjointed; energy dissipates. Without an aim, the captain has no idea where to steer the pointy end of the ship; without an aim, the builder cannot pour a suitable foundation; without an aim, the speech maker's speech is just a stream of disconnected words and phrases. And the result? The ship crisscrosses the open sea, the building is susceptible to high winds and earth tremors, and the speech evokes no heartfelt emotion and provokes no purposeful action. We wander.

Our story begins with an aim: all display monitors meeting specifications. Rose wants to create an operation that doesn't involve waste. It's an exciting idea. There's a certain heroism involved. Can it be done? They will have to take some risks, and they don't know what will happen. They'll need to pull together. But there is doubt; the inspection mentality kicks in, "If you want all display monitors to meet specifications, you'll have to lower the standard."

Rose is asking the assembly line workers to stretch and grow, to learn and create anew. The key line is, "We'll improve the process so that all monitors meet specifications." The aim requires action: the workers need to study the assembly process. They need to learn in order to create. Also, in order to generate significant improvement, Rose needs to bring together the people who work *in* the process to work *on* the process. The aim must be shared. Finally, having achieved their aim, the workers forge a new one, "to make all display monitors exceptional." In the race for quality, as the Xerox advertisement so keenly states, there is no finish line.

The scene shifts from a factory floor to a university with a dean saying, "We won't change the expectations. We'll change the process so that all students can meet the expectations." Again, there is the challenge. Why shouldn't all students succeed? Why can't we make exceptional learning unexceptional? Why isn't excellence in teaching the norm? And again, there is the excitement of being involved in a great and wonderful dream—something special, something that will set the unit or institution apart, something that people can brag about.

How many colleges or universities have such an aim? Very few. Indeed, most institutions rely on printed vision statements, that is, long-winded discourses that string together a series of flowery references to excellence. Within each category (e.g., liberal arts colleges, research universities), you could easily "white out" an institution's name in its vision statement and substitute another school's name. Few people would know the difference because few institutions have a unique, compelling aim that helps drive individual initiative and foster cooperative work.

There are exceptions. There are institutions with vision statements that reflect a shared aim and inspire the concerted action advocated by the dean in our story. Rio Salado Community College, a "college without walls" in Phoenix, Arizona, is one:

> Rio Salado Community College is the college of choice for our students because we guarantee the opportunity for academic success through excellence in teaching, competency based curriculum, and student shared responsibility for learning. Our responsive and responsible commitment to our students and communities is evident through accessible student services, innovative learning design and convenient delivery, supported by advanced technology. As leaders in total quality, we foster a supportive and collaborative academic and work environment based on equal opportunity that empowers each individual.

How does an institution work toward an aim like this? How do you create something new? A vision statement, presented on handsomely bordered paper, is one thing; changing a culture, developing a force in people's hearts, is something quite different.

The key to substantive organizational change is the alignment of an organizational aim with process goals and individual commitment. Processes (series of activities that create outputs) are how work gets done in an organization. If the goals of work processes do not relate to the aim, nothing really changes. There is a vision statement and there is work, but they are not connected. Further, processes are designed, implemented, staffed, and managed by people. The rewards and sanctions embedded in their jobs, as well as the values they share with each other, determine what actually gets done.

Back to the factory floor. Things changed—"A new paradigm. A new computer company."—because there was alignment. Things changed because the process was studied and then redesigned to meet a new aim that Roger, Michele, Teresa, Laura, and Rose (who was responsible for bringing them together) bought into. Without all three—the vision, the process goals, and the individual commitment that create a shared aim—alignment does not occur and things remain pretty much as they have always been.

How about Rio Salado's vision? It looks good. In fact, it looks great in the front of their college catalog. But does it make a difference? It already has. Much of the credit goes to Rio Salado's leaders, who built the vision from the bottom up. The aim was shared from the beginning because it emerged from personal visions. Peter Senge, in *The Fifth Discipline*, does a marvelous job of explaining that a vision is only as effective as the process by which it is developed. At one point, he quotes an industry executive who says, "My vision is not what's important to you. The only vision that motivates you is your vision." Pursuing that thought, Senge goes on to suggest that organizations intent on building shared visions continually encourage their members to develop their personal visions. (Lesson 14, "Spread hope," explores this issue from the notion of personal involvement.) If people don't have their own vision, all they can do, according to Senge, is "sign up" for someone else's. The result is compliance, not commitment.[4]

Rio Salado engaged in an iterative process to promote sharing. First, the college's 20-member steering committee used an affinity diagram (a tool used to identify relationships within large amounts of data) to draft and organize a series of sentences that reflected the kind of organization committee members were interested in creating. Two- and three-person teams from the steering committee then went to units throughout the college and asked individuals to reflect on their jobs.

The teams asked, "How can you make your own job better? Can you see that job in this vision?" And then, "If not, why not?"

The responses were gathered, and the committee refashioned the vision. Then the teams went out again, "Better?" they asked. The committee exercised its vastly improved wordsmithing skills one more time. The resulting vision statement was put in the catalog, but it also appears on all the computer screens at Rio Salado as phrases that move across the screen when individuals check their electronic mail. The original version has changed three times in three years. The vision statement evolves as the hopes and dreams of aspiring faculty members, staff, and administrators evolve.

But how about the work? How has the work changed? One example will do. Rio Salado has no campus. It operates 250 off-site classrooms and employs many adjunct faculty members. How can you "guarantee the opportunity for academic success through excellence in teaching . . ." with part-timers? The first thing Rio Salado did was scrap peer review in the teaching evaluation process. The college is moving, instead, to a teaching portfolio approach, designed to identify the best practices in teaching and learning and encourage the sharing of those practices and the continuous improvement of the faculty in the aggregate. If the aim is teaching excellence, all the work processes that have an impact on the quality of teaching, such as the performance evaluation system, need to align with that aim.

Steven Covey, the leadership expert, uses the compass as a metaphor for moral reasoning.[5] He often speaks and writes about the importance of a compass in turbulent times. As the water swirls and the winds shift, it is critical to have a stable landmark—one that provides a true north. It is just too easy to get blown off course without one. A minor squall pushes you in one direction, a strong current pulls you in another. Chaos ensues; reactivity abounds. In the wink of an eye, you can convince yourself that building more jails will make you safe, that handing out more F's will improve the quality of education.

I think we can all agree that higher education is hip-deep in rough seas and turbulent times, so the first lesson of this book is particularly appropriate. Whether you're considering a display monitor production line, a Rural Sociology program, or a community college in Phoenix, Arizona, the place to begin is with the end. Significant improvements in quality and productivity do not just happen. They don't involve luck or rely solely on the words of an inspired leader or the actions of dutiful followers. There needs to be a methodology that teases out simple truths and sharply defined aims. Such a methodology must engage people in a dialogue to nail down what is truly important and fashion a riveting, compelling, and widely shared vision of what tomorrow can be. We need to begin with an aim—a true north—that becomes the driving force for all that we do.

QUESTIONS

What does your institution or unit consider important?

How often, and in what manner, do you or the institution reflect on those aims?

In what ways are those aims reinforced? In speeches? In policies? In behaviors?

Ask 20 people—administrators, secretaries, professors—what is most important to them in their work. Do their answers resonate with stated institutional or unit aims? If not, why not?

LESSON 2

> "Left to our own devices, we pay too much attention to things of too little importance to the customer."

Michael Kiner, a first-semester sophomore at the local community college, decided that he wanted to test out of Geometry 210. It was a required course for his major, Respiratory Therapy, but Michael had done really well in high school geometry. His younger brother was taking the class in high school now, and every time Michael helped Bob, the material came back to him easily. Three weekends with a textbook was all that Michael would need.

__Monday, 9:20 A.M.__ Michael enters the Medical Technology office and asks the secretary how he goes about taking the Geometry 210 exam. She directs him to the Admissions and Records office.

__Monday, 9:40 A.M.__ The line in the Admissions and Records office is short. Michael waits for about five minutes, then asks the woman behind the counter how to take the test. She gives him a credit-by-examination form and tells him to fill it out and return it to the Liberal Studies office. He takes the form and heads off to his 10:00 Advanced Writing class.

__Monday, 2:15 P.M.__ After lunch, Michael takes the completed form—name, rank, social security number—with him to the Liberal Studies office. The secretary tells him that the form needs to be reviewed and approved. He can return tomorrow afternoon.

Tuesday, 3:25 P.M. There are a few students ahead of him in the Liberal Studies office. The secretary digs his form out of a small pile of papers. She tells him that it has been approved. He needs to take the form back to Admissions and Records, but he's anxious to get home and study for a test the next day.

Wednesday, 8:30 A.M. Bright and early, Michael returns to the Admissions and Records office. He presents his ap-proved credit-by-examination form to the same clerk from Monday. She says that her office needs to determine whether the GPA and completed-unit requirements have been met. He should return tomorrow.

Thursday, 10:10 A.M. Michael is back in the Admissions and Records office. Judy, the clerk, informs him that all the requirements have been met. He is then told to take the form to the Educational Services office in order to have a section number assigned.

Thursday, 10:30 A.M. A person in the Educational Services office assigns the number and directs Michael back to the Admissions and Records office. He'll have to wait until after his 11:00 class.

Thursday, 2:20 P.M. Michael registers for the geometry course in the Admissions and Records office. His now good friend Judy tells him that he needs to return to the Liberal Studies office to arrange to take the examination.

Friday, 3:50 P.M. The secretary in the Liberal Studies office pulls out a large calendar. She and Michael go over some dates and settle on three weeks from Friday.

Friday, 4:00 P.M. Michael walks to his car and heads for home. Maybe he'll stay in tonight. He's tired; it's been a long week.

❖❖❖

The customer—the person who uses or benefits from the output of a process—plays a key role in improving quality because it is the customer who defines quality in the first place. There is universal agreement on this point. The user, not the producer, ultimately decides whether a product or service has value. We see validation of this principle all around us: the automobile buyer, not the automobile maker, casts the final quality vote; the theatergoer, not the actors, decides whether a show is a hit or a miss; the patient, not the doctor, judges whether a particular treatment relieves the pain.

The vital role of the customer in quality improvement is perhaps best summarized in the Malcolm Baldrige National Quality Award. The award is given to U.S. manufacturing and service companies and small businesses that excel in quality management. The award criteria are built upon a set of 10 core values, the first of which is "customer-driven quality." This core value is described, in part, in the following manner:

> Quality is judged by customers. All products and service characteristics that contribute value to the customer and lead to customer satisfaction and preference must be the focus of a company's management system. . . . Customer-driven quality is thus a strategic concept. . . . It demands constant sensitivity to emerging customer and market requirements, and measurement of the factors that drive customer satisfaction and retention.[1]

The winners of the Baldrige—Milliken, Ritz-Carlton, Motorola, and others—often testify to the importance of customer-driven quality in the revitalization of their enterprises, and their healthy bottom lines validate their testimony. Indeed, if you visit the shop floor at Motorola or stay the night at a Ritz-Carlton hotel, you can see that the rhetoric of customer-driven quality is not mere fluff and frill. The people in these organizations think and act differently, and we, as consumers, respond accordingly. We become brand loyalists and word-of-mouth advertisers.

So, why does the concept of customer cause such angst on college campuses? Why do some college administrators regard the notion of customer as an evil influence that sullies and undermines the lofty aims of their institutions? Why do some professors, armed with a sense of indignation, think it is necessary to challenge anyone who utters the word *customer* in their presence? And why, when speaking in a campus setting, do quality management advocates often encounter a back row of professors and administrators squirming in their seats, using the communication art known as body language to express their intransigence on the subject? Why is that?

These behaviors could be dismissed as defensive reactions to change, and, no doubt, some portion of the negativity and hostility is just knee-jerk cynicism. (See also lesson 9, "To create the future, challenge the past.") That reaction, however, explains only a tiny fraction of the expressed concerns. There is no real reason to believe that higher education has a greater percentage of cynics than health care, financial services, or any other industry. (Our cynics may be more articulate, but, proportionately, we have only our fair share.) The real explanation is much more profound and surprisingly complex, and we must understand these driving forces if we expect to have any hope of helping institutions become more responsive to the needs of those they serve.

I believe there are five campus-specific factors that greatly influence the way we think about our customers. The first two involve the competing roles that professors play: (1) professors were customers before they were professors, and (2) professors are often their own best customers. The next two factors are organizational in nature: (1) colleges are functionally oriented, not process oriented, and (2) colleges have multiple and competing customers. The last factor involves the nature of those who benefit from our output: students do not behave like customers.

Language is a powerful influence in our lives. As people learn a particular language, they acquire a distinct set of tools to relate, analyze, and function in their world. G. Clotaire Rapaille, the cultural anthropologist, has paid specific attention to the link between emotion and language development in his work.[2] Language lets people grasp the meaning of objects, actions, and relationships. Learning language, according to Rapaille, is not passive. It is an active process, relying on personal discovery and grounded in emotion. The result is an imprint, a permanent pathway that links words with an emotional experience. It is at that level—a deep, intensely personal level shaped by experiences—that a word, even a word like *customer*, has its most profound meaning.

College professors were customers before they were professors. They have played that role most of their lives, from a six-year-old buying an ice cream cone to a 40-year-old purchasing a home. They know what it means and how it feels to be a customer. Most important, there is an imprint associated with the word, an imprint that I believe evokes an emotional response along the lines of "the customer is always right."

When the notion of customer-driven quality is introduced into the academy, every professor and many administrators (who have been professors) are forced to reconcile their customer imprint with the three little letters that follow their surname—Ph.D. A terminal degree is exactly that, terminal. There is no more: no higher, no better. Indeed, the word *doctor* has its own imprint that involves connotations and meanings associated with the superlative. So, at the language level, how does a professor or administrator handle the notion that the student, or industry, or society, or even another professor is their customer? Understandably, they don't deal with it well. A customer is right—always right. That means contol and influence. It means that others stand in judgment of them. The word *customer*, and its accompanying imprint, is the oil, and the word *professor* is the water; at a very basic linguistic level they simply do not mix well.[3]

A professor also has the difficulty of reconciling the role of knowledge creation and knowledge dissemination. As knowledge creators, professors are engaged in research and original thought. This intellectual development is not only personally satisfying, it is usually the major component of their employer's reward system. For example, in spite of

the pounding rhetoric for increased emphasis on undergraduate education, tenure decisions are still made largely on the basis of academic
scholarship. And who is the key gatekeeper of the tenure process? The
senior professor down the hall.

The result, again, is that a professor has difficulty in reconciling these
two competing roles. On the one hand, there is the role of knowledge
creator (researcher), which emphasizes specialization and contempla-
tion; on the other hand, there is the role of knowledge disseminator
(teacher), which emphasizes generalization and integration. As professors get better at the former (the role they are being rewarded to
excel at), they accentuate the gap between their own intellectual development and that of their students, who are, supposedly, the primary
customers of the educational enterprise.

From an organizational perspective, the word *customer* is a struggle
as well. Higher education has a strong functional orientation that reflects a focus on the organizational chart. There are two customer-re-
lated problems that necessarily result. One is that people own boxes,
not processes. Without ownership and leadership, there is no one to
help direct people's attention to the goal of the process, which should
entail customers' expectations. Second, with no encouragement to look
to the user of the output for requirements, most people instinctively
look to the person who issues sanctions and disapproval for directions.
A "look outward" orientation is replaced by a "look upward" orientation. In general, the notion of the customer loses much of its signifi-
cance when the notion of process is not understood.

Another organizational factor involves multiple constituencies. If we
stick with a definition of customer as "anyone who uses or benefits
from our output," we quickly see the problem that colleges and universities face. Apple focuses its efforts on particular consumer segments
of the computer-buying market and Southwest Airlines seeks to carve
out a niche among air travelers. Who can legitimately lay claim to the
services of an institution of higher education? A short list would include local businesses, community groups, accrediting agencies (both
regional and specialized), state educational officials, and athletic pro-

gram supporters and fans. Of course, there are also current students, prospective students, and former students, not to mention the parents, spouses, and employers of these students. And those are just the external customers. A director of admissions, for example, operates in a supplier/customer relationship with every academic department, all of whom have a wish list for the quality and quantity of incoming students.

Higher education is a customer-intensive environment. Faced with a stream of forceful and competing demands, many people on a college campus feel overwhelmed by it all. Customer voices are ignored as faculty and administrators retreat in frustration to the friendly confines of their respective pigeonholes on the organizational chart. In effect, we are soaked with customers but thirsty for a customer orientation.

The final factor involves our primary customers—the students, themselves. They pay thousands of dollars for a service that is supposed to enhance both their quality of life and their capacity to earn a living. Usually, there is a strong, positive return on their investment, but not always. Sometimes they get a professor who is ill prepared, sometimes their program of study is poorly designed and does not focus on appropriate competencies, and sometimes advisers give them bad advice. In most of these situations, students act more like well-mannered employees than well-informed customers. They don't complain, and they don't make demands. The result is predictable: if students don't behave like customers, why should they be treated like customers?

What do all of these factors have to do with Michael, the bedraggled college sophomore in our story? The inability of a college or university to develop and practice a customer-driven orientation results in both ineffective (Michael cannot be pleased about his action-packed week) and inefficient (needlessly complex and wasteful) processes.

Let's review precisely how this happens. First, all the professors, administrators, and staff members who have a hand in the design and delivery of credit-by-examination see themselves as the professionals they are. They are highly skilled; Michael is not. The "customer is always right" imprint kicks in. How could Michael be the customer? He's just a Med Tech student. What does he know about credit-by-examination that we, the experts, don't already know? Next there is the issue of where professors' attentions are directed. Even though credit-by-examination is an integral part of the academic delivery system, how many professors are intimately involved in its design and continuous improvement? What do you think has a bigger payoff for a professor, redesigning the credit-by-examination process or having an article accepted by a prestigious journal? Again, the culture and the reward system suggest to any sane professor that his or her primary customers are other professors, not students like Michael.

From an organizational perspective, while Michael is certainly the primary customer of the credit-by-examination process, there are other customers or stakeholders as well. The Liberal Studies office, the Admissions and Records office, and the Educational Services office are all secondary customers because they exist in a supplier/customer relationship with each other. Every time there is a handoff, one office is benefiting from the previous office's work. (Lesson 5, "An organization is a relay team; the better the handoffs, the better the results," deals with this issue in detail.) Into this mix of service providers and users we can also stir the various supervisors from each of the offices. Each of these individuals has a political interest in the process that has been sliced and diced three ways; in effect, there is no owner for the credit-by-examination process.

The result is that the primary customer of credit-by-examination is the supervisor within each office, the secondary customers are the office personnel, and Michael—well, Michael is a very distant third. Why? Because what happens if several credit-by-examination forms slip through the Liberal Studies office without being approved? The supervisor will express his or her displeasure to the office personnel. In contrast, what happens if the credit-by-examination process takes a student, like Michael, one week of trans-campus excursions to complete? Nothing. Again, why? Because peoples' upward-looking orientation on a college campus is reinforced by the fact that students act more like employees than customers. Like employees, they rarely complain about their treatment. So, Michael keeps his mouth shut and makes his daily rounds. The office workers, in turn, continue to look to their supervisors for rewards (and try to avoid sanctions), while ignoring the unexpressed needs of the 19-year-old in the sweatshirt and ripped jeans standing at their desk.

Focusing on the end-user is not a hokey, feel-good tag line to be put on coffee cups and motivational posters. It is not just fashionable rhetoric. By deciding who the primary customers are and what their requirements are, we can establish process goals, outputs that are need-satisfying. With such goals in mind, we are then able to design a process that effectively and efficiently meets those goals. Further, management is able to develop appropriate process measures, allocate requisite resources, and facilitate effective handoffs such that outputs can be continuously improved. The goals of the process, defined in terms of customer requirements, become the unifying influence that drives process design and aligns management practices.

One of the best descriptions of customer-driven design is offered by Joseph Juran.[4] Starting from his definition of *quality* as "fitness for use," Juran articulates a sequence of steps that he refers to as "the quality planning road map" for improving performance. The first three steps in the plan are:

1. Identify who are the customers
2. Determine the needs of those customers
3. Translate those needs into our language

He spends over 50 pages in his book *Juran on Planning for Quality* describing in great detail the ways to identify customers, the varieties of customer needs, and the processes that most effectively translate customer language into organizational language. The remainder of the road map has seven steps including those for establishing units of measure and optimizing process design and capability. The essential point is that identifying, determining, and translating are the action steps needed to establish process goals which, in turn, are the enablers of process design. It's the riveting focus on the end user that is critical.

A similar approach is offered by the leading practitioners in the reengineering movement. *Reengineering* is defined as the fundamental rethinking and redesign of processes to achieve dramatic improvements in performance. The driving force behind a reengineering effort—and why it is such a hot topic in a broad range of organizations—is not incremental improvement but a quantum leap in performance via paradigm-smashing innovation. In order to do that, you begin with a clean sheet of paper and ask yourself, If I could start all over, would the process I design look like the current one? Oftentimes the answer is no. So, where does a reengineering effort begin? The leading experts in the field are quite clear in their answers. According to Michael Hammer and James Champy, "The best place for the reengineering team to begin to understand a process is on the customer end. What are the customers' real requirements?"[5] Thomas Davenport, another reengineering advocate, counsels that a correctly designed process "has the voice and the perspective of the customer 'built in.' "[6]

The point is that whether the goal is incremental improvement or radical innovation, the design of processes, or how the work gets done in an organization, should be driven by end user requirements. When it is not, the process (like credit-by-examination) degrades into one that operates for the convenience of the people who work in the process, rather than for the customer of the service—"Left to our own devices, we pay too much attention to things of too little importance to the customer."

In higher education, the redirection of attention to customer-driven quality can yield tremendous gains in both effectiveness and efficiency. For example, the University of Houston—Clear Lake (UHCL) is currently "reinventing" its Masters in Public Management degree program. Enrollment figures had been down, yet there was a large, potential market of some 20,000 scientists, engineers, and other highly trained professionals within the UHCL enrollment area. In short, the university had a degree program without a market and a market without a degree program. UHCL began holding a series of discussions with key members of the Clear Lake aerospace community in an effort to develop a "strategic intent" or vision. The question they were attempting to answer was "What is the picture we should have in our minds of what students graduating from this program should be like (competencies, character, attitudes, values, and so on)?" An initial finding was that the most frequently mentioned management skills that members of this community would need in the future were "understanding the business of our business," "having interpersonal or people skills," and "understanding the public-private or government-industry interface." With these and other customer-driven requirements in mind, UHCL is beginning the instructional redesign. Without that focus, however, the chances are great that any curriculum revision would still reflect (as it always has at both UHCL and every other college or university) the singular interests of individual departments and professors.

At Delaware County Community College (DCCC), a similar design approach is being taken with the course scheduling system. The vice president for collegiate instruction organized a team to recommend ways to make the system more effective and efficient in light of increasing demands on limited facilities and services. He identified four goals:

1. To refine the definition of customers and suppliers for course scheduling
2. To establish quality characteristics for course scheduling in consultation with customers and suppliers
3. To develop and administer assessment tools that will measure the degree to which quality characteristics have been met
4. To recommend changes to the processes that will enable the course scheduling system to meet or exceed customer needs within the limits of available resources

DCCC is responding to a process that had decomposed into one that served the self-interest of a series of disconnected people. By renewing a commitment to understanding the nature of supplier/customer links, the college has a real chance at designing a class scheduling system that is much more responsive to its customers' requirements.

At Miami University a team of professors has been working to create empowered learners in the classroom by sharing control—in effect, to view the student from a customer perspective in which the service of teaching and learning becomes a joint responsibility of both.[7] The model seeks to align student goals with faculty goals, thereby forging a partnership that yields stronger learning outcomes. For example, the first several days of classes are spent not on content, but on process, that is, "reacting to syllabus," "generating class requirements," and "understanding self assessment and the nature of feedback." By creating a collaborative climate, in which students have the opportunity to shape the nature of their work, the Miami team has found that students perceive the resulting assignments to have greater meaning and relevance. The key is to fashion an open, creative environment in which both the faculty member and students understand the aim and are motivated to contribute to its success. Miami's student-as-partner approach to the design and delivery of educational services is, again, one that seeks to overcome the natural tendency of processes to degrade into self-serving practices of questionable effectiveness. In the classroom, such degradation usually leads to some form of the "stand and deliver" model in which the professor stands in front of a class and delivers whatever he or she pleases.

This lesson—"Left to our own devices, we pay too much attention to things of too little importance to the customer"—illustrates the predicament that higher education finds itself in. Developing an orientation that views quality as a function of the service user's perceptions, not the producer's, is difficult for campus dwellers. We have significant language, organizational, and control issues to overcome, but we need to do it. We simply cannot afford to respond to customers' needs in inefficient and ineffective ways, such as those prominently showcased in the "highly aerobicized" process Michael was forced to negotiate to register for Geometry 210.

The credit-by-examination process at Michael's institution needs to be redesigned. Moreover, the redesigning needs to begin with a direction-setting end in mind that focuses on customer expectations, just as University of Houston—Clear Lake is doing with its masters programs, Delaware County Community College is doing with its class scheduling system, and some faculty members are doing with their classes at Miami University.

QUESTIONS

Who are your customers? That is, who uses or benefits from your output?

How often and in what manner do you solicit their requirements?

How do you use such information to redesign your work processes?

How do you coordinate your work with other departments to design and carry out customer-pleasing processes?

PART 2

PROCESS DESIGN AND MANAGEMENT

PERFORMANCE IMPROVEMENT FRAMEWORK

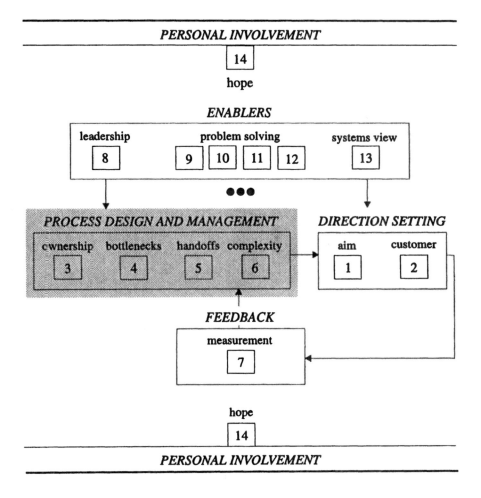

LESSON 3

> ## "Waste is the unintended consequence of unattended work processes."

Tom Gayton made a note on the sheet, put it in the pile to his right, and then said, "There you go. Thanks," to the student peering through the small window. He took a quick glance at his watch, then looked at the long line that stretched out before him. His eyes shifted and refocused on the next student. "Hi," he said. The student, an Asian woman in her late twenties, said, "Hi. It's nice to finally get to the front of the line." Tom could certainly relate. "Yeah, it's been like this all day."

Tom went through the checklist. First he looked on the computer for "holds"—library fines, traffic tickets, and so on. Then he checked to make sure the classes were still open and whether there were any required signatures for things like advising or course prerequisites. The last course—Chinese Literature (CHN 310)—was a problem. There was a prerequisite listed; the student had not taken it and didn't have a waiver.

He explained to her what she would have to do. It involved a hike over to Baumann Hall on the east campus. "Do I have to get back in this line?" the woman asked, as if to say, take my money, take my car, but please don't make me get in this line again. Tom wished he could say, "No. Don't bother. Just drop it in the box over there," but that wasn't the way the system worked.

❖

*Lynn Yi hustled out the door. She needed to pick up the kids
at the day care center by four. That was in an hour. She
thought about taking the campus shuttle bus but decided to
half-walk, half-run to Baumann Hall.*

*How did she miss the prerequisite? And why was there
one anyway? She was born in China and came to this
country when she was eight. Her college major, somewhat
surprisingly, was English Literature, but in the process of
reading Chaucer, Fielding, and Hardy she thought it would
be interesting to study the works of her own heritage.*

*It took her 20 minutes to reach Baumann Hall. The De-
partment of Asian Studies was on the third floor, down the
hall, to the right.*

*There was a knot of students standing around a small table
placed next to the office doorway. Behind the desk was a
woman, about Lynn Yi's age, flipping back and forth in a
computer printout. Next to the printout was a rubber stamp.*

❖

*Susan Sullivan had been a secretary in the Department of
Asian Studies for almost five years. In the beginning her
work was easy. There were eight professors, with the usual
typing, filing, and answering phones. In the last few years,
however, the work load had seemingly doubled. The department had developed a series of courses to support an Asian
concentration in the business school's International Business
major.*

*The student in the front of the line said he needed an
advising stamp. Susan stamped.*

*There was a similar initiative with the Political Science
Department. An Asian concentration was being developed
for the International Affairs major, and several new courses
were being offered this semester on an experimental basis.*

The next student in line needed a stamp, too.

Susan had asked for additional help. Maybe a work-study student several hours a day. So far, no deal. The budget was too tight according to the department chair.

Susan smiled at the next person in line. Her left thumb and forefinger went automatically to the pages of the print-out. Let's see, CHN 540 . . . 340 . . . there it was, CHN 310. The prerequisite was ASN 200—Asian Cultures. Susan didn't really have to look for the professor's name listed next to the prerequisite. She knew it was Wu. She also knew that there was no Professor Wu, at least there hadn't been one since she had been there.

This always happens, she thought. The professor listed next to the prerequisite either wasn't on campus during registration, didn't teach the course anymore, or—in one or two instances—didn't exist.

Susan looked at CHN 310 again. There was plenty of room and the woman was Asian. She grabbed another waiver form—just as she had done for a dozen other students—and wrote in the name "Lynn Yi." Then she grabbed the stamp and made the waiver official.

❖

"The green's about 160 yards from here," remarked Barry Oldham. "It'll take a full four iron to make it." He was on the fifth hole of the Mission Hills country club golf course. William Wu stepped out of the golf cart and slid a three iron from his bag.

William knew a four would never make it. He also knew that Barry knew it would never make it, but it was a running joke they had going back six years. That's when he, a newly retired professor from northern California, and Barry, a retired cop from Chicago, were first matched in a foursome.

William strolled over to the ball, took a few practice swings, then took a hard cut. Damn. The ball was hooking wildly over onto the next fairway. William was lost for a moment in despair—thousands of dollars of golf lessons

flashed before his eyes—then he had the presence of mind
to yell, "Fore!" to the unsuspecting couple walking down to
the eighth hole.

❖❖❖

Let's begin with a few definitions from the lesson "Waste is the unintended consequence of unattended work processes." First, waste is that which adds cost without adding value. Another way to say this is, waste is the ratio between efficiency (minimizing the resources used) and effectiveness (producing the desired results). An important aim for an organization, therefore, would be to manage its waste aggressively, to add as much value to its products or services, while minimizing the resources used.[1] Such an aim would be as appropriate for UCLA and Swarthmore as it has been for Motorola and Ford.

A second definition. A process is a method for doing things. Using inputs, individuals perform a series of activities. As a result of these activities, something or someone is transformed, resulting in output. An organization is only as effective as its processes and systems.

A final definition. Unattended means that the process has no owner and/or is not being monitored. A process owner is an individual charged with the responsibility for the efficiency and effectiveness of a process. Mere ownership, however, does not guarantee that the process is being monitored—with established control points, defined measurements, and feedback loops—so that the process can be modified or corrected. In practice, what often happens is that sections of a process have one or more individuals doing work activities. These individuals, in turn, have a supervisor, but supervision of a section does not equate to ownership or responsibility for the process. When the extended process, from supplier to end user, is not owned by a single individual, the process is said to be unattended.

Now, why do unattended processes produce waste? The problem begins when you lift the lid of an organization and peer inside. The first thing you see is the organizational chart, not the system or its processes. You see boxes with neatly centered titles. In higher education the chart would have a president or chancellor; a series of three, four, or five vice presidents; a line of deans and directors; and so on. The functions in the chart show the reporting structure—the vertical view—but that's not how the work gets done. A different perspective is offered by a horizontal, or systems/processes view of the organization. This view focuses on cross-functional processes. For example, curriculum management and faculty hiring are key processes in higher education, but you won't see either on any college's or university's organizational chart.

A process orientation has tremendous implications for an organization. An entirely different thought pattern occurs when you focus your emphasis on processes rather than organizational structure. The differences extend to how problems are analyzed, how opportunities are pursued, and how resources are allocated. A process-savvy mind-set is centered on learning and improving, while a functional approach is invariably forced to "fix things."

A dramatic example of these differences is detailed in the following comparisons adapted from the work of H. James Harrington:[2]

Organizational focus	Process focus
• Employees are the problem	• The process is the problem
• Do my job	• Help to get things done
• Measure individuals	• Measure the process
• Change the person	• Change the process
• Can always find a better employee	• Can always improve the process
• Motivate people	• Remove barriers
• Control employees	• Develop people
• Don't trust anyone	• We are all in this together
• Who made the error?	• Reduce variation
• Understand my job	• Know how my job fits into the total process

While a process focus is clearly a superior methodology for improving quality and productivity in an organization, it must be understood that this is not a minor variation on a more traditional management theme. A process approach is not merely a shift in language or a minor change in individual responsibilities. It is a very different and much more demanding way of operating an organization. A functional perspective assumes a static environment with an emphasis on individual job descriptions and vertical reporting lines. A process perspective, in contrast, assumes a dynamic environment and recognizes that processes have virtually nothing to do with boxes on a chart. That's not how the work gets done. A process perspective also validates an important reality: processes get better or worse; they rarely stay the same. No matter how well they are initially designed, processes that are not actively and aggressively managed degrade over time. They are not self-sustaining, continually reinventing themselves to meet new challenges and changing conditions. Processes that are not monitored, like the prerequisite process described in the story, will necessarily begin to produce waste by adding more and more costs and less and less value. It is inevitable.

A simple example. A new car is put into service by a car rental agency. As a system, it is in perfect condition: the engine is tuned, the chassis lubricated, the tires balanced. Now, disconnect the monitoring mechanisms—the oil pressure gauge, the temperature gauge, and so on. Further, every time the car is rented and returned, put it back out to be rented and returned again. What happens? There is no owner, just a bunch of people who have access to the system and its processes. There are no control points, measurements, or feedback loops. The processes are unattended, and the natural, unintended consequence, is that the system (the automobile) and its processes degrade. No one person is at fault, yet, within months, the car will cost more to fix than it is worth.

Organizational processes, like those in our rental car, also change when left unattended. They begin to misfire and run rough. Lines lengthen, mistakes become commonplace, and morale begins to sink slowly like the sun in the western sky. Necessary modifications aren't made because no one is watching and no one is responsible. Everything is someone else's job. Finally, the process begins to be reshaped. Slowly and inevitably, it takes on a different form than was originally designed. But the process does not change for the best interest of the organization or the end user—the customer; it changes for the convenience of the people in the process.

Our story is illustrative. Having prerequisites for courses is a good idea. The aim is to help students accumulate basic skills before moving on to higher-order learning. The requirement not only facilitates learning, it facilitates teaching. In effect, it improves the educational system. When the process functions well, a professor can be confident that all the students who attend his or her first class meeting possess minimally acceptable skill levels across a range of critical competencies. The acquisition and demonstration of this prerequisite knowledge is a process with inputs, value-added transformation, and output. That output, in turn, becomes the student learning input upon which the professor can build additional learning that leads to another output. This cycle continues throughout a student's academic career.

Unfortunately, the process can also have an unintended consequence—waste, or that which adds cost without adding value. Where is the waste? Let's begin by identifying the value that is being added in the process. In Lynn Yi's case, there is none. The output of the process is a stamp. A stamp without meaning. At what cost? There are the costs of Tom and Susan's time and of developing, copying, and distributing forms. By themselves, these costs are not terribly significant. But the real problem is that we don't know whether Lynn's experience is an isolated incident or whether most of the bleary-eyed students standing in Tom and Susan's long lines are caught up in the same or similar non–value-added work processes. If so, the costs may very well be significant. Moreover, there is at least a possibility that other departmental secretaries across the campus are sitting at little hallway tables, stamps in hand, begging for extra help (and some getting it) because they are overworked.

Why is this process producing so much waste? The answer involves management. There is none. The process is unattended, and even the most logical and well-behaved process can't manage itself. An unmanaged process

- Can't establish goals that serve to focus people's attention on the future.
- Can't develop and monitor measures so that performance can be improved through feedback. (This is the subject of lesson 7, "Measurement without feedback is just data; feedback without measurement is just opinion.")
- Can't determine the resources required for the process to achieve its goals.

The issue of an unattended process is particularly problematic (and, therefore, particularly wasteful) when the process is cross-functional. If a process falls within the narrow confines of a box on an organizational chart, there is real hope that it will be managed. Hope quickly fades, however, when the process is cross-functional. A useful illustration is the curriculum management process. Who actually manages curricula at most colleges or departments? Professors own their individual courses, but who owns the process that cuts across the courses and defines a degree program? Who is responsible for the process's effectiveness and efficiency? In fact, there are a series of *who* questions that apply to curriculum management or to any other cross-functional process on a college campus:

- Who monitors process performance and reports periodically about how well the process is meeting customer requirements and internal goals, as well as about indications that the process is becoming inefficient and ineffective?
- Who ensures that a permanent team continuously improves process performance?
- Who facilitates the resolution of interface problems among the functions that contribute to the process?
- Who develops the process plan and budget?
- Who serves as the conscience and champion of the process?[3]

Many people might respond that the roles just enumerated describe a director's or dean's or department chair's position. But do they? How many chairs, say of a Sociology department, know who the different customers of their degree program are and their requirements? How many deans of arts and sciences work with professors to ensure that courses are sequenced correctly, learning outcomes for each course are clearly identified, and those competencies match customer requirements? How many have a process plan for continuous improvement?

A good example here is the work being conducted by the Department of Music at Xavier University.[4] The department's consciousness was raised after studying U.S. Department of Education data that showed only 19 percent of recent graduates with visual and performing arts degrees were employed full time in a job closely related to their field of study. In effect, performing arts students invest large sums of money and critical early years of study in professional arts preparation, yet experience an almost 80 percent failure rate in terms of job acquisition/placement. Xavier thought that it could do better. Certainly each professor was doing his or her job, but the program—the extended, cross-functional process—was on automatic pilot.

The department began studying its own program in opera education and concluded, "Something is clearly sub-optimal in terms of costs and value of opera performers' education. . . . " The department attributed its own shortcomings to the fact that no one was responsible for the education process and no one questioned the outcomes of the education process—the process was unattended.

The department has since reorganized the management of its operations and has redesigned its opera education program based upon one goal, "To facilitate output of optimally prepared performing artists, in appropriate numbers, to meet industry needs." In order to achieve this goal, the new Xavier model will

- Provide performer education based on detailed knowledge of current and changing opera performer requirements as defined by opera management

- Address changing student needs and expectations and incorporate enrolled students in continuous redesign of the education process
- Measure outcome success and plan continuous improvement both for enrolled students and for the opera education process using statistical tools and methods

Recently, the history department (60 faculty members and 10 staff members) at the University of Wisconsin—Madison (UW), engaged in a similar bit of soul-searching. The chair of the department, with the help of several internal university consultants, reviewed some of the department's staff and process difficulties. For example, the process for proposing a new course or changing a course title filled five pages. There was a great deal of seasonality in staff jobs, so some staff members were underutilized while others were overworked. Also, the department filled staff vacancies without considering changing needs (consequently, the department had plenty of typists but no one specifically trained to provide computer support). Taken together, these issues reflected a management problem: No one was responsible for coordinating and improving the staff's work processes.

The department chair persuaded the university and the state to apply an especially high-level classification to an open departmental secretary position. The position, educational services assistant, requires a college education, significant supervisory experience, and subsequent professional training in management. The new person does not devote significant time to doing traditional office tasks. Instead, she is responsible for serving as an essential link between faculty and staff, teaching staff to work in teams, helping staff understand how their jobs fit within the department's mission, and allocating resources to help fulfill that mission. The historians at UW have managed a paradigm shift in the staff support area from one that focuses on the organization to one that focuses on processes and ownership and improvement of those processes.

Finally, there is a certain irony in our opening story about prerequisites. There are three key elements common to any production process: transformation, feedback control, and repeatability. Output is fundamentally the result of one or more transformations (e.g., physical, locational, transactional, or informational). Feedback involves a means to modify or correct certain attributes of the output. Repeatability implies that a process is executed numerous times in the same manner. William Wu, the phantom professor at the end of the story, engaged in his own process at the golf course. He hit the ball and provided locational transformation, a process he intends to repeat up and down 18 holes. The errant shot, however, can produce an outcome of unintended consequence—a beaned fellow golfer. It is fortunate that Wu's process has a feedback control element: eyes to watch the ball and a mouth to yell "Fore!" when the process starts going out of control.

It's unfortunate that Lynn Yi and her classmates aren't so lucky. The unattended process they are caught up in will continue to degrade like our rental car, producing waste and gobbling up scarce resources without adding real value to any educational outcomes. In contrast, the students in Xavier's opera program and the faculty and staff in the history department at UW are lucky. They may not know it yet, but the quality of their educational experiences and work lives is about to change for the better. That is because improvement is not assumed in these two academic programs; it is owned.

QUESTIONS

Enumerate and describe the key processes within which you work.

What are the goals associated with those processes and how is success measured?

Who is responsible for ensuring that the people who work in the processes work together to improve continuously the performance of those processes?

LESSON 4

"The capacity of a system is limited by its bottlenecks."

Rhonda loved her work in the Grants and Contracts office. It was exciting, challenging, and rewarding. As an administrator she worked with professors throughout the university in developing proposals—from a $2 million grant for AIDS research to $5,000 for studying the costs and benefits of debeaking chickens.

But today, Thursday, it was anything but exciting. Instead, it was draining and debilitating. She had been working with Professor Connell Cowan for the last six months on a major grant proposal for the National Cancer Institute. Professor Cowan, an immunologist, was the principal investigator, but there were five other professors intimately involved in the research study from three other departments. The research methodology was extremely complex and it had taken them two months just to work through the details of the final draft.

The problem was the deadline. It was tomorrow, Friday.

In spite of working almost around the clock for three weeks, it had come down to the last few days. On Monday morning Rhonda ran a quick mental inventory of the people who had to approve the proposal. There were the three department chairs and the dean. There were also the vice presidents: her boss (the vice president for research and graduate studies), the vice president for academic affairs, and, finally, the vice president for administration.

Seven signatures.

Campus mail was completely out of the question.
It would take three weeks. The pony express could do better.

There was a work-study student in the office on Monday morning, so Rhonda sent him on a mission: track down the department chairs and get signatures. Rhonda made it a point to come in early on Tuesday and meet the dean before he went into a meeting. That left the vice presidents. She got her boss's signature before 10:00 A.M., then swung by the vice president for academic affairs' office just before lunch.

For the remainder of Tuesday and all day Wednesday, she tried to reach someone in the vice president for administration's office. The telephone either rang or Jody, the secretary, would put her on hold.

By Thursday, Rhonda was panicking. She decided to walk over to the office—220 Sullivan Hall.

❖

Esther had worked in the housing office for 15 years. When she had started, there had been only three dormitories. Now there were six. They began working on the latest one in January of this year.

The contractor had assured everyone that the dorm would be ready in July. Well, here it was September—one week before freshmen and new student orientation—and there were still dozens of details needing attention. In some rooms doors still needed to be hung, and other rooms needed touch-up paint.

For Esther, though, the biggest problem was the keys. Last week the contractor had dropped off the room keys, four sets for 85 rooms. She had called up university stores to get another key rack but had been told they were out of stock. That meant she would have to requisition one from a local office supply warehouse.

*The real problem, unfortunately, wasn't the requisition: it
was the cost, $27. Everything over $25 had to go through
the requisition process, and that meant three signatures and
probably two weeks' worth of time.*

She didn't have two weeks.

*So Esther did the only thing she could do—"walk it
around." She managed to get two signatures quickly, but the
last would be a problem. It had been before—220 Sullivan
Hall.*

❖

*Jody came back from lunch a little after 1:00 P.M. She turned
the corner to walk into the her office and bumped into a
tired-looking Rhonda, from Grants and Contracts. She had
arrived mid-morning and was still there. In addition to
Rhonda, there were three other people. Jody recognized
one—Esther from housing—in the hallway. Esther and one
of the other women were seated in chairs; the others stood.*

*As Jody pushed opened the door labeled "220," she knew
exactly what to expect—people seated in the two chairs
inside the office.*

*All these people trying to "beat the system" by walking
around papers to be signed had really become a problem.
Jody's boss, David Kaminsky, hated a crowded or cluttered
office area and had mentioned it to her on two or three
occasions during the last few weeks.*

*Jody decided to take action. On a notepad she scribbled a
reminder to herself to order two more chairs for the hallway.
That should just about do it.*

❖❖❖

The Goal, a novel by Eliyahu Goldratt in which the hero is a plant
manager facing the imminent closure of his factory, is a thoroughly
unlikely combination—a thriller about production and operations management. Early on in the novel the hero's boss makes a statement in a

meeting that serves to push the plot for over 300 pages, "The future of our business depends upon our ability to increase productivity."[1]

Productivity, the ratio of output to input, reflects the efficiency of internal operations or how well resources are used in a system. To improve productivity you need to improve work processes, either by increasing their capacity and, hence, their output capability or by reducing the amount of resources required. The greatest gains are made when both actions occur simultaneously. There is one additional twist that is pointed out in *The Goal*: productivity is meaningless unless you know what your goal is. This seems reasonable, especially given what we learned from the first lesson—"Begin with the end in mind." The aim in the first half of that story was to make all display monitors "exceptional." So, every action that brought Roger, Rose, and the rest of them closer to that aim was productive. In a highly competitive global economy such a focus on goal-driven efficiency is critical to survival, but does it follow for our colleges and universities? Does it make sense to pursue a more productive teaching and learning environment?

I believe that the current conundrum facing higher education officials in the state of California sheds some light on the answer. According to demographic projections, California's colleges and universities must accommodate an additional 450,000 full-time students by 2006. To meet this demand, state support for higher education will have to increase by 52 percent in real terms—that is, from $5.8 billion in 1991 to $8.7 billion in 2006. That means higher education's slice of the revenue pie will need to increase or the pie itself will need to increase. Neither is projected to happen. It seems that public schools, welfare, health care, and corrections have crowded to the front of the budget line. And the pie itself? Estimates are that California's economy will have to expand at a real rate of almost 3 percent per year to match the funding needs of the almost 1.5 million additional students. Unfortunately, the economic growth rate over the past 12 years is less than half that rate.[2]

The response of colleges and universities in the state system of higher education to this specter of impending doom has been painfully predictable: raise student fees, cut purchases of supplies and equipment, defer maintenance, eliminate some part-time teaching positions, and save through a series of early retirements.

Patrick Callan and Joni Finney of the California Higher Education Policy Center, an independent organization created to stimulate discussion and debate about the purposes and goals of California higher education, summarize the dilemma in the opening statement of a 1993 report: "California's public higher education as historically and currently organized, delivered and financed will be unable to accommodate projected enrollment demand over the next 15 years." They add, "If our state officials and university administrators continue to ignore this problem by focusing almost solely on budgetary issues, the future of educational opportunity for the citizenry of California is likely to be one of slow erosion."[3]

Does the issue of productivity have a place at the table of higher education? Given the California situation, which is being played out to a lesser degree in many states across the country, the answer must be yes. Increasing the efficiency of our work processes is the only way to ensure that more students succeed with fewer resources. One could easily do a little word play with the opening quotation from *The Goal* and be pretty close to the mark: "The future of higher education depends upon our ability to increase productivity." In effect, we must do more teaching, learning, and research with the same or even fewer resources.

Given our definition of productivity, most California institutions are becoming more productive. They have reduced the denominator in the ratio, the level of inputs, through their various cost containment efforts. If the numerator, the output, remains the same, there will necessarily be some improvement in productivity because the math has changed. But the gains are likely to be disappointing to most people other than bottom-line budget analysts. Early retirement programs— the drug of choice for bottom-liners—are a perfect illustration. The budget is no doubt reduced by such programs, but studies indicate that when a lucrative buyout plan is offered, the more productive people tend to leave. They have new projects, new plans for their time.[4] The numbers are changed, the institution is downsized, but the ability (or inability) of the system to convert input into output remains the same. Such programs are, in effect, perfectly designed to transform larger, inefficient institutions into smaller, inefficient institutions.

The real equation for improvement is maintaining or slightly decreasing the amount of resources while significantly increasing the capacity of processes to produce output—that is, more with less. The *more* part of the equation is a brain teaser; the *less* part is just a Sunday stroll in the park. Anyone can cut equipment purchases or lay off workers, especially when there is a mandate from the board or the state treasurer's office. It is no intoxicating challenge to impose a 10 percent across-the-board budget cut. Increasing capacity, however, means improving the capability of work processes, which is far dicier than passing out pink slips. People who work in the system must find a way to increase the rate at which the system or its processes produce output, a metric that's referred to as throughput. For a manufacturer, such as our computer company, throughput is the rate at which the system generates finished products. For a college or university, throughput is the rate at which the system generates research, service, and learning.[5]

So, exactly how do you increase capacity? The answer is found in an area of operations research known as constraint theory. One of the main precepts of constraint theory is that throughput is limited by the system's bottlenecks. A bottleneck, in turn, is any resource whose capacity is less than the demand placed upon it.

In *The Goal*, the hero struggles to understand this concept in his manufacturing plant with little success. One weekend he goes hiking with a troop of 15 Boy Scouts who are bursting with energy but burdened with knapsacks and sleeping bags. Over the course of the morning, the plant manager has to call repeated halts because of gaps in the line. It doesn't seem to make any difference whether he marches at a steady pace from the front or yells encouragement from the back, the line spreads out and boys are either running to catch up or stopping to wait for the others. After watching this scenario unfold again and again, he concludes that, except for the first person in line, everyone else's speed depends upon the speed of those in front of them. The hike is a series of dependent events. Moreover, the rate at which they walk the trail—the throughput—is governed by the slowest kid in the troop. In this case, it is a fat kid named Herbie.

Herbie is the bottleneck. He has the least capacity for walking, so he becomes the rate-limiting factor for the troop. The solution is to put Herbie at the front of the line, then figure out a way to help him go faster, to increase his capacity. They do it by redistributing his knapsack load. Each troop member increases his load slightly and Herbie, lighter by 20 pounds, is able to lead them down the trail at a new and improved rate of speed.

In our story, 220 Sullivan Hall is Herbie. It is a bottleneck, a rate-limiting factor that impedes throughput and, consequently, reduces productivity. How can it be otherwise? The vice president, David Kaminsky, signs for everything, from million dollar grants to $27 key racks. His personal style demands control. The institutional policies reflect this inspection mentality. With each additional signature, with every added procedure, the bottleneck tightens and the people begin to stack up, first in the office, then down the hallway. The scarce resources of the institution—in this case, the brain power and work ethic of its employees—are wasted on Esther's vacant stares and Rhonda's frustrated pacing.

An institution interested in improving its performance must search for bottlenecks and then work hard to increase capacity. Unfortunately, most colleges and universities respond to bottlenecks the same way that Jody in 220 Sullivan Hall responded: they order more chairs for the hallway. They confuse cause and effect. Their attention is diverted to the immediate, the obvious, while the root cause of the problem remains untouched and undeterred from continuing to damage the efficiency of the institution's operations. But not all institutions have the same response to bottlenecks. Some have caught on to the importance of maximizing throughput and are responding to the difficult challenge of doing more with less. Let me share two illustrations, one from the administrative side of a university, the other from the academic side.

The Department of Telecommunications at the University of Kansas (KU) is responsible for maintaining the telephone systems on the 30,000-student campus. The department routinely received complaints about its slow service, in spite of the fact that the department was fully staffed. After analyzing the entire work order process and soliciting information from its customers, a telecommunications team concluded that the culprit was the work order form itself. According to team members, "Our work order flow chart showed many holding patterns that were a direct result of a lack of information and a need for further clarification on the form. Too much time was spent deciphering improperly filled out work orders." They concluded, "The form simply did not ask the right questions."

One of the obvious indicators of a bottleneck is a concentration of unprocessed work. With Herbie it is a clump of Boy Scouts stepping on his heels; with 220 Sullivan it is a phalanx of chairs in the hallway. At KU there was a knot of work order forms in various stages of rework. Indeed, by conducting a study, the department discovered that three out of four forms required additional information before actual work could be initiated. Again, the response to a similar scenario in our story was to put more chairs in the hallway. The equivalent at KU would have been to ask for an additional work-study student to help manage the holding pattern of rework.

Instead, the team began a series of brainstorming sessions, consulted with other institutions, and redesigned the form. Team members then conducted a trial run and recalculated the amount of additional information that was requested. It was 29 percent. The nearly 50 percent reduction in rework expanded the capacity of a bottleneck. Throughput increased, but resources did not.

Now the academic application. Curriculum management is the single largest process at most universities. It encompasses advising, career counseling, developing plans of study, curriculum planning, and course scheduling. At George Mason University (GMU), a working group on service improvement generated a list of major complaints about the process. The list included the following:

- Approximately 10 percent of students applying for graduation have not met requirements because of unavailability of courses, closed sections, or inaccurate information about degree requirements.

- Many students cannot graduate in the nominal four-year span because courses they need as prerequisites are offered infrequently or are full.

- Many students request and receive special exceptions and waivers to substitute courses for others that are not available. Processing these requests occupies much faculty and staff time.

- On the first day of classes, many faculty members find themselves confronted with students who could not register because the class was full and who request permission to register.

In addition to this, a survey of nonreturning undergraduates—students who attended GMU in the fall of 1992 but not the spring of 1993—revealed that nearly half said that "difficulty getting wanted or needed courses" was either a major or minor reason for not returning.

There is an obvious recurring theme here: unprocessed work concentrated in front of a bottleneck. The effect of having crowds of students trying to squeeze through the bottleneck of required classes is predictable. Some of the work-in-progress offloads itself; students transfer to other institutions. Some of the work-in-progress tries to circumvent the bottleneck by requesting special exceptions and waivers for required (but full) courses. Still other work-in-progress causes a commotion by simply showing up on the first day of class, whether registered or not (a phenomenon that students across the country refer to as "crashing a course").

The George Mason problem highlights two fundamental characteristics of bottlenecks that are important for higher education institutions. First, an hour lost at a bottleneck is an hour lost for the entire system.[6] In effect, a loss at a bottleneck is nonrecoverable. The student who can't get into the required course (and who doesn't transfer, wrangle a waiver, or crash the course) must try again the next semester. Productivity falls off because throughput (the rate of goal-directed learning) decreases. The loss can't be recaptured because the bottleneck is the rate-limiting factor. The result: "Many students cannot graduate in the nominal four-year span."

Second, an hour saved at a non-bottleneck is a mirage. What happens when George Mason University, or any other university with a similar curriculum management bottleneck, decides to move to a touch-tone registration system? What happens when a professor is allowed to teach what is believed will be a popular new course elective—say, "Rock Stars as Role Models." In the first case, a three-day registration process is reduced to one day; in the second, additional credit hours are generated by the speech communication department. Neither of these improvements will have any effect on throughput or the rate at which the student generates required competencies. That rate is solely governed by the bottleneck produced by the ineffective curriculum management system. The high-tech registration does have the benefit of informing students in record time that they still can't get into the classes they need to graduate, but "Rock Stars as Role Models" may keep them entertained on Tuesday and Thursday afternoons.

There is every reason to believe that the university within which Rhonda, Esther, Jody, and David work is having the same budgetary problems that other institutions are having. At the precise time that six people are crowding into the tight confines of 220 Sullivan Hall and spilling over into the hallway, the president may very well be arguing for more resources at the state capital. The sad irony is that if the president is successful, productivity will likely decrease. Again, the math tells the story. The chances are that the new-found dollars will be applied across the board—a little deferred maintenance, a modest increase in departmental budgets. Throughput is not affected because bottlenecks such as 220 Sullivan Hall, indecipherable forms, and over-subscribed classes remain solidly in place. The denominator increases, the numerator does not. And the ratio that measures the efficiency of the operations, productivity, inches slowly downward.

QUESTIONS

Audit your work processes. Where is work-in-progress stacked up?

Again, what is the aim of the system or processes?

Given that aim, what can be done to relieve the tightness that is causing the bottleneck? How can you, along with others in the process, work to spot new bottlenecks as they appear and then smooth them out?

LESSON 5

"An organization is a relay team; the better the handoffs, the better the results."

It began with an innocent question. Nothing earth-shattering. In fact, it was the kind of simple question that often gets answered with, "I don't know."

"I was in the supermarket and a professor I know said, 'Hi!,'" comments Casey, the director of facilities and maintenance at a midsize eastern university. "We exchanged pleasantries and discussed the probability that it would rain for a fourth straight day. That was about all. But, then, just as she started to push her cart around the corner, she looked back and said, 'Casey, how come we can find the money to build a new recreational facility but I can never find any chalk in my classroom? Why is that? It drives me nuts.'"

It was almost an afterthought. Certainly nothing to lose sleep over. After all, Casey was in the midst of two major renovation projects, not to mention trying to get the new recreational facility ready for fall semester. Chalk? There was plenty of chalk. Wasn't there?

On a whim, Casey decided to do a little survey. "It certainly wasn't anything fancy. Just a few questions on a postcard," he said. "Our janitorial staff helped develop it. The janitors left a postcard on every professor's desk when they cleaned offices at night. All the professors had to do was drop the cards in the campus mail. Well, the results were pretty amazing to me.

"All of us shared the impression of professors as being finicky, fussy, and demanding, but there were only three things that really bugged them: burned-out light bulbs, unemptied trash cans, and—you guessed it, right there at the top of the list—no chalk in their classrooms."

Casey decided to dig a little deeper. He asked professors, he asked secretaries, and he asked janitors. "Tell me about chalk," he asked. And he listened.

The professors said, "There's usually no problem, but every once in a while I walk into my class two minutes before the period is to begin, and there are only bits and pieces of chalk. Then I have to run to the classroom next door or down the hall to my office. I always keep a box in there for emergencies."

The secretaries said, "Occasionally, professors will come flying in here just before their classes looking for chalk, so we keep an emergency supply."

The janitors told another story. Although "resupplying chalk" was one of their duties, there were several different approaches. Some janitors said, "I just put a couple of new pieces out each night." Others said, "I wait until there are a few short pieces left." Most janitors put new pieces of chalk on the ledge of the chalkboard, but quite a few put a full box of chalk in the desk drawer. If they were late, some admitted they didn't bother replacing chalk at all, because professors had their own chalk, as did the department secretaries.

Casey and a few of the janitors decided to figure out a better way to resupply chalk. They met with someone from carpentry and designed a chalk dispenser. It looked like a straw dispenser, made out of wood with a Plexiglas front, so it was easy to see how many pieces were left. The dispenser held a full box of chalk and attached to the wall next to the chalkboard.

And the result?

The professors stopped asking their secretaries for an extra box of chalk because chalk was where it was supposed to be—in the classroom.

The secretaries stopped ordering extra chalk because no one ever asked them for it anymore.

The janitors started worrying about only one thing, keeping the chalk dispenser full at all times.

And Casey began looking for other chalk-like opportunities to make real improvements.

❖❖❖

What's the big deal here? In a decade of tough budget cutbacks and spiraling tuition rates, when public trust is down and public expectations are up, why would anyone bother to write about chalk? So there's no chalk. So it takes a professor a few extra minutes to locate some every once in a while. So what?

The answer is that chalk is a requirement for professors. It is one of the things, along with a roomful of well-prepared students, a chalkboard, and good lighting, that professors need to perform a series of activities. Chalk, therefore, is no different from any of the multitude of inputs individuals in a college or university require to do their work: the dean of Arts and Sciences needs financial data from the budget office to allocate resources, the Graduate Office needs departmental recommendations to extend an offer of admission to an applicant, and the chemistry professor needs sulfuric acid from university stores to conduct experiments. Chalk—or, in this case, the lack of chalk—is a symbol. The degree to which the chalk is where it is supposed to be, when it is supposed to be there, has an impact on the effectiveness and efficiency of the individual professor and, in turn, the institution. The better the handoff, the better the result.

An organization is a relay team because as the organization transforms input into output it relies on a series of handoffs between internal suppliers and internal customers. One of the best ways to improve organizational performance, then, is to improve the handoffs. Unfortunately, the practice of better handoffs is a lot more difficult than the discussion of better handoffs, especially when the organization is a college or university. One explanation for higher education's problem in this area is detailed in a set of linked propositions:

1. Academics are consummate barrier builders
2. Institutional barriers restrict communications
3. A lack of communication ensures that specific customer/supplier requirements are never discussed and agreed upon
4. The lack of agreed-upon requirements results in poor handoffs that are wasteful

Let's begin with the building of barriers. One of W. Edwards Deming's famous 14 points is "Break down the barriers between staff areas."[1] Deming argues that organizations build barriers between units that make it difficult for individuals to see the overall process in which they are involved. The result of this compartmentalization is the "tossing it over the wall" phenomenon Deming described seeing at Ford Motor Company. Each unit at Ford did its work separately, hunkered down behind a series of walls, without communicating with other units. The resulting lack of perspective had a disastrous effect on the process as a whole. The design team worked hard to develop a design it believed was a winner and tossed the design over the wall to manufacturing, which did not have the tools necessary to make the car as designed. Manufacturing retooled for the complex design, which raised the cost of the car, and then tossed the design over the wall to marketing. The salespeople were asked to sell a vehicle whose increased cost of manufacturing pushed the price beyond the target market. The end result was disappointing sales.

There are many reasons for the type of barrier building described by Deming. Howard Gitlow and Shelly Gitlow, in their analysis of Deming's work, suggest the following as contributors to an extensive network of barriers that separate and isolate people and units in an organization: competition, personal grudges, different ways of looking at a problem, different priorities, ignorance of an overall mission, increased emphasis on specialization, and certain organizational structures.[2]

A college or university is the institutional equivalent of a honeycomb. Our culture promotes separateness; our policies encourage the building and nurturing of inviolable cells. Consequently, admissions officers talk to admissions officers, librarians to librarians, and the advising staff to other members of the advising staff. There is the hard division between student affairs and academic affairs, along with the age-old gap between administrators and professors. Nowhere, however, is the organization more fragmented than between and among the academic units.

Recently, William Massy, Andrea Wilger, and Carol Colbeck highlighted the issue of faculty isolation and fragmentation with their research into the conditions within departments that support or inhibit faculty members' working together on undergraduate education. Of the three key features that constrain faculty collaboration in teaching, the primary constraint is fragmented communication patterns resulting from the atomization and isolation of faculty members. The major causes of fragmented communication that emerged from the researchers' interviews were

- Autonomy: "Overwhelmingly, our respondents identified a central reality of academic life: faculty work alone."
- Specialization: "As one faculty member noted, specialization is the route to publication, which, in turn, determines tenure, promotion, and salary increases."
- Civility: "We have avoided fighting and discourtesy. We have kept up a facade of good manners at the cost of not accomplishing much."
- Generational splits: "Differences among the generations were cited repeatedly by faculty as a powerful and divisive force."

- Personal politics: "The polarization is so intense, in fact, that some faculty 'perceive each other as good or wicked depending upon their ideological stance.' "[3]

Barrier building and a lack of communication, then, go hand in hand. The effect is predictable. As I noted earlier, every employee of a college or university requires inputs to transform or convert into outputs, e.g., financial data into resource allocation, departmental recommendations into admission offers, and sulfuric acid into experimental results. When barriers are built and communication is restricted, however, the precise nature of customer requirements is never discussed. The budget office, for example, doesn't ask the dean's office about the best way to present financial data; the dean's office, in turn, never attempts to sit down with the budget office and make its preferences known. Neither overtly recognizes the supplier-customer relationship, so there is no attempt to identify and embed the "voice of the customer" into the design and delivery of the service.[4] Instead, the financial data get tossed over the wall, along with the departmental recommendations and the sulfuric acid.

Without the voice of the customer—the person who uses or benefits from the output—the work of the supplier tends to become self-serving. As discussed in lesson 2, "Left to our own devices . . .", suppliers do what they think is best, or what they like, or what their immediate superiors like. The result is a predictably poor handoff, a mismatch between what suppliers provide and what customers expect. Scrap, rework, complexity, breakdown, and delay—all forms of waste—are possible consequences of bad handoffs. Oftentimes, a whole new layer of bureaucracy emerges to deal with scrap and rework. Shadow systems spring up, the rationale being, "If they can't do what we need, we'll have to do it ourselves" (e.g., department-based financial spreadsheets are purchased). Poor input can throw a system out of sequence and cause delay by simply not being there, according to specification, when needed (e.g., admission offers are late, experiments are delayed).

In summary, barriers create poor communications, which, in turn, mean that the supplier never understands the customers' requirements.

Because of misunderstandings, the handoffs are sloppy, resulting in waste, and waste is a measure of low quality and poor productivity.

Our chalk story ties it all together. There is an obvious barrier. The chances are slim that the janitors see their work as being in any way connected to the teaching and learning process. They are janitors, not professors. Janitors work at night, professors work during the day. Some janitors speak broken English; most professors speak excellent English. The effect is that there is no communication between the two groups. It should come as no surprise, then, that faced with significant barriers and no communication, the importance of chalk to professors escapes the janitorial staff. It should also come as no surprise that given little understanding of the professors' requirements, the resulting handoff is poor. Sometimes there is chalk, sometimes not. When there is no chalk, the process breaks down (separate stashes) and teaching time is lost as professors search for something to write with (waste).

Again, the availability of chalk may seem inconsequential when measured against the grand scope of higher education, but the lesson—"An organization is a relay team; the better the handoffs the better the results."—has broad implications for our institutions. At Pennsylvania State University, for example, a 10-person team of engineering and physics professors has been meeting every two weeks since the spring of 1992.[5] Why? The first part of the answer involves the recognition, on the part of the deans of two colleges (science and engineering), of the importance of one particular course. Physics 201 is the traditional introduction to general physics, the first of three physics courses required of all engineering majors. Physics 201 covers the basic principles of classical mechanics such as motion, energy, and gravity in a four-credit course that meets twice a week in a large lecture setting (300 students) and twice in smaller (30 students) recitation sections. Three sections are offered, enrolling a total of 900 students each semester. Given the numbers involved and the critical nature of the prerequisite material being covered, it was obvious to the two deans that this was a critical handoff.

The second part of the answer is that the handoff was perceived to be not only critical, but also flawed. For example, some engineering professors believed that their students had not sufficiently mastered the material contained in the introductory physics course. Instead of teaching new material, the engineering professors were having to review basic physics. Even when students were good at the "plug and chug" of solving mathematical equations in physics, they often had difficulty applying the concepts to practical engineering problems. Finally, there was the concern, shared by both physics and engineering professors, that introductory physics had become a "weeding out" exercise. Grades for the course were on a curve with mean exam scores often in the fifties and sixties. Some freshmen became so discouraged by their experience that they switched from science or engineering to majors in other fields.

The physics-engineering handoff problem should not be surprising. After all, the barriers at Penn State are as structurally sound as they are on any other campus: the departments are in two different colleges in two different buildings; the physics courses are lower-division and the engineering courses are upper-division; and the disciplinary emphasis in engineering is on application, while the emphasis in physics is split between theory and practice. These barriers and others made it difficult for physics professors and engineering professors to recognize their unique supplier-customer relationship. Engineering professors did not communicate a set of "physics competencies" to the physics professors, and the physics professors did not ask. The result: bad handoffs. How do we know? Rework. Engineering professors had to spend time teaching remedial physics, both concepts and applications. Then there was scrap—another form of waste—evident in the rate at which students were being "weeded out."

In the almost three years since the professors began meeting, the team has implemented a variety of measures, including surveys, tests, and interviews, to learn about faculty perceptions, student satisfaction, and student learning. They have used the information to develop a variety of innovations to enhance student learning, such as the following:

- More laboratory opportunities have been added
- Training of teaching assistants has been upgraded with the hiring of an instructor whose job is TA supervision and with the creation of a TA "tips" booklet
- A study strategies guide has been developed and given to all students in the introductory physics course
- At-risk students are now identified via their scores in the university's freshman testing program and are given the opportunity to enroll in a one-credit preparatory course

The formula is clear. Reduced barriers lead to increased communications—professors begin talking to one another. Expectations are discussed, common problems are tackled. The supplier-customer link becomes manifest and a partnership is formed. Everyone benefits from an improved handoff: the professors, the students, the institution, as well as future employers.

A final observation. Having established the causes and effects of poor handoffs, is it not necessary to fix the blame? Wasn't the lack of chalk the janitors' fault? It can't be that hard to ensure that chalk is available. And at Penn State clearly the engineering professors were at fault. They never established or communicated their expectations. It is difficult enough for a physics professor to teach the laws of thermodynamics to a bunch of 20-year-olds without also having to master the art of mind reading. So, who is at fault? No one, really. But who is responsible? That answer, in all cases, is management—the administration.

In a previous lesson—"Waste is the unintended consequence of unattended work processes"—I emphasized management's critical role in counteracting the tendency for processes to degrade. Unattended work processes, like automobiles, begin to run rough as minor misfires go undiagnosed and performance measures are not used to inform necessary changes. Scrap, rework, complexity, breakdown, and delay are the inevitable price of such inattention. The set of linked propositions described earlier in this lesson adds a demanding twist to management's role in improving quality and productivity. The propositions suggest that a disproportionate amount of waste is generated at the handoffs, so it follows that a disproportionate amount of management's attention should be devoted to handoffs. The shift from a functional focus to a process focus requires a shift from owning a box to assuming responsibility for what happens between the boxes—the white spaces on the organizational chart—as the two deans at Penn State have done.

What we are really talking about in this lesson is the creation of highly synchronized organizations. As we have seen, the contribution of any single person to the organization's aim is very much dependent upon the performance of others. The organization cannot succeed with a whole series of runners sprinting off in all different directions. They must work as a team with clean handoffs. Teamwork can occur only if barriers are reduced and communication is increased. Some refer to this process as moving toward a "seamless" organization (the antithesis of a "toss-it-over-the-wall" organization). Others say that we need to get out of our boxes and begin to manage actively the "white spaces on the organizational chart."[6] It is difficult for individuals working within the processes to do this. The individual janitor or physics professor does not have the cross-functional perspective, the incentive, or the authority to engage in organized barrier busting. Management does, and the degree to which management helps bring individuals together to discuss their handoffs is the degree to which the institution can produce winning results: efficient processes and effective outcomes.

QUESTIONS

What are the things that you require of others in order to do your job?

How much time and energy do you spend fixing those things when they are not right?

Who are your suppliers? That is, whom do you depend on for the input?

How often and in what manner do you communicate your requirements?

For administrators: To what degree do you encourage and facilitate dialogue between customers and suppliers in your unit and across units?

LESSON 6

"In the absence of a search for the unnecessary, complexity drives out simplicity."

Catherine Lynch first saw the smiley face in January when Anna, her assistant director, wanted to schedule a three-day vacation. It was on a form that had "Request for Vacation or Absence from Office" emblazoned across the top. There were lines for name, purpose of request, dates, signature, and so on. The bottom of the page, which was sectioned off, also had a signature line, under which was typed "Director, Office of Institutional Research." To the right of the signature line were two faces, one with a smile, the other with a frown.

Catherine asked the secretary, "What's this?"

Mary Jean explained. The previous director had developed the form to make sure the office was properly staffed at all times. There was a master calendar on the computer. Anyone who was going to be away checked the master calendar and retrieved a form from the supply closet. The form was submitted to Mary Jean. She, in turn, passed it along to the director. The director reviewed the request, checked the master calendar, and then checked the appropriate face. The director gave the form back to Mary Jean, who made a copy. The original went into a file; the copy was sent back to the person making the request.

*After six months of checking smiley faces, Catherine had a
blinding flash of the obvious. Yes, it was important that the
office be covered, but this wasn't the emergency room at
Kansas City Memorial Hospital; the reports and studies
weren't life-or-death decisions. Besides, there were only 10
people in the office, and everyone seemed to check the
master calendar before filling out a request form. Any
problems were resolved among the staff before the form was
filled out. So, what was the purpose of the form?*

*At the next department meeting, Catherine led a discus-
sion of what was meant by adequate staffing. The group
came to a consensus, and everyone discussed how the
master calendar could best be used to ensure adequate
staffing. Then Catherine stated that, unless anyone had an
unusual passion for smiley faces, she really didn't see the
point in filling out a form.*

*On her way out the door at 5:00, Mary Jean went to the
supply room, gathered up the now-obsolete "Request for
Vacation or Absence from Office" forms and, smiling all the
while, deposited them in the paper recycling container at
the end of the hallway.*

❖❖❖

Complexity is a general term for unnecessary work. Most of us have
barely enough time to do what is absolutely essential, so why would we
spend time doing unnecessary work? Why would we perform tasks that
make a process more complicated without adding any value? The answer is that complexity is usually not designed into a process; it seeps
in over time.

We begin with a simple process, such as one for hiring adjunct faculty members. The hiring process is standard for all departments, has
five steps, involves three offices (budget, personnel, and the academic
department) and three signatures, and takes 10 days to complete. It is
neat and clean. Then slowly, incrementally, things begin to change. A

separate affirmative action office is created, reporting directly to the president. An extra step is added in the budget office because several departments had a problem living within their means. The board of governors develops a new reporting guideline to comply with federal immigration laws. The newly hired vice president for academic affairs decides she needs to approve all offers, tenure-track or otherwise. Each year another "well-intentioned" bell or "necessary" whistle is hung onto the process. In the end, everyone complains about the Rube Goldberg process that requires 12 signatures and 65 days to complete.

There will always be complexity. It is impossible to eliminate all un-necessary or non–value-added work. As complexity increases, however, the time available for value-added work decreases. In a previous les-son—"The capacity of a system is limited by its bottlenecks."—the bottle-necks acted like a crimp in a hose. The capacity of the process was reduced and productivity, in turn, decreased. The effect that needless complexity has on a process is identical: productivity decreases. The cause, however, is different. The existence of an unnecessary "Request for Vacation or Absence from Office" form or a 12-signature hiring process doesn't act as a crimp in the hose; it acts as a leak. Scarce re-sources (in the form of inputs such as employee knowledge and time) are squandered on the inconsequential and unnecessary. Like the wa-ter that escapes through a leaky hose, the energy and skills of individu-als are wasted doing non–value-added work. Output, especially customer-pleasing output, necessarily declines.

A more direct look at the core critical process of higher education, learning and teaching, illustrates the full nature of the insidious ef-fects that unnecessary complexity has on productivity. For a number of years, William Massy and Robert Zemsky have drawn our attention to what they call the deconstruction of the undergraduate curriculum.[1] They contend that over the last two decades, as faculty members have pursued specialized knowledge in their disciplines, there has been a shift away from required courses. Rather than taking courses in an ordered sequence, students must develop their own sense of how the various elements of knowledge fit together. The deconstruction of the curriculum has had important economic consequences in terms of course proliferation and the need to hire more faculty (especially adjunct faculty members to teach core required courses that are abandoned by tenured professors in pursuit of more exotic interests).

The increased fragmentation of faculty work life and the nonsystematic nature of curriculum changes have increased complexity in four ways: (1) mistakes and defects, (2) breakdowns and delays, (3) inefficiencies, and (4) variation.[2] Let's look at each of these curricular complexities in greater detail.

When mistakes occur, there is usually an attempt to fix them. Rework adds cost to the production of products or services. Sometimes a defect cannot be repaired, so it is eliminated. Scrap adds cost, too. What types of mistakes and defects result from the curriculum deconstruction described by Massy and Zemsky? The obvious problem is poor academic performance. With course proliferation and minimal sequencing, students can easily end up in courses for which they are ill-prepared. When they perform poorly, they sometimes take the course over. If the problem occurs in their major, they may switch to another major. In some circumstances, students may drop out of school or transfer. In all cases, the resulting mistakes and defects are the institutional equivalent of a leaky hose.

The second type of complexity is breakdown and delay. There is little predictability in the system described by Massy and Zemsky. Take the basic shift away from required courses, stir in a steady mix of new courses, add a splash of poor advising services, and you have the perfect recipe for a planning and economic nightmare—the inability to match supply and demand. The system suffers from significant oversubscription of some courses while the professors of other courses hawk their classes in the student newspaper and on bulletin boards trying to avoid a dreaded cancellation notice from administration. Before long a four-year degree becomes a five-year degree as students bounce from one closed-out course to another. Given a constant set of resources, if the time taken to graduate increases by 25 percent, the productivity of the system necessarily decreases by 25 percent.

Inefficiencies result from using more time, energy, or materials in a process than are absolutely necessary. A deconstructed curriculum generates many inefficiencies. For example, when the content of one course is developed without regard for any other course, a student may easily be exposed to the same concept—say, Maslow's hierarchy of needs—over and over again. Like our notorious "Request for Vacation or Absence from Office" form, the time spent rehashing Maslow for the fifth time is an inefficiency that is manifested by a classroom full of students engaged in window-gazing, doodling, and daydreaming instead of being actively involved in value-added learning.

Variation, the final form of complexity, is a particular problem in the learning and teaching process. One can argue that too little variation is a problem. A lockstep series of courses with standardized teaching methods might be too focused on producing graduates that think and act alike. On the other hand, too much variation is a problem as well. Every college or university professor has launched into a spirited discussion of a topic, such as the effects of the Crimean War on the diplomatic relations of Austria, only to realize that half the class—the half with the knitted brows—has never heard of the Crimean War. The professor is then forced to add steps to the process—a short capsule summary of the conflict in spite of the fact that Nineteenth-Century European History was supposedly a prerequisite for the course. Curriculum deconstruction increases variation because most professors have little knowledge of the base competencies of their incoming students each semester.

Again, as complexity increases, throughput and productivity decrease. Scarce resources are tied up doing non–value-added work. Such work—filling out useless forms, tracking down extra signatures, teaching concepts that should have been covered in earlier coursework—leaves less and less time for value-added activities that would meet or exceed the expectations of customers. The effect is not unlike the image painted by the words of the English satirist Jonathan Swift. Both Gulliver and the body of the educational enterprise are slowly but surely immobilized by thousands of constraints of Lilliputian proportions.

The lesson for this chapter—"In the absence of a search for the un-necessary, complexity drives out simplicity."—implies that a certain innocence accompanies simplicity. Indeed, it would be nice if we could keep things simple, but the reality is that things get messy. No one orchestrates complexity; no single person is culpable. It just sort of happens, one small constraint, one little breakdown at a time.

The lesson also implies there is a methodology that could aid us in the virtuous battle against complexity, and there is. A process can be seen as a "value chain." Each step in a process, by its contribution to the creation or delivery of a product or service, should add value to the overall process. The greater the ratio of value-added steps to non—value-added steps, the greater the productivity and, in turn, the greater the competitive advantage of the organization.[3] The best way to iden-tify unnecessary work is through value analysis.[4] Value analysis consists of analyzing each step in a process to evaluate its importance in achiev-ing goals. The first question to ask of any activity is "Is it necessary to achieve the goal?" If the answer is yes, then the activity is business value-added work. It is a fundamental requirement of the organiza-tion and cannot be eliminated. The second question is "Does it con-tribute to customer requirements?" If the answer to this question is yes, the activity is customer value-added work. It is an expectation that directly influences how the customer perceives the quality of the ser-vice rendered.

We can use our story as an example. In this case, the primary goal is the adequate staffing of the Institutional Research (IR) office. People in the IR office who are planning to take vacation or be absent from the office first check the master calendar and enter their vacation or intended absence on the calendar based on what they see. Is this activ-ity necessary to achieve the goal? Yes. Everyone in the office needs to know what everyone else is doing to ensure adequate staffing. Does the activity contribute to customer requirements? The users of IR in-formation and analysis expect people to be in the office to answer their questions. The master calendar contributes to that customer require-ment, so checking the calendar is customer value-added work as well.

Now, is the "Request for Vacation or Absence from Office" form necessary to achieve the goal? Maybe. For example, intended absences may need to be reported to an agency or board. If so, the answer could be yes. Does the form contribute to customer requirements? No. Customers are not interested in back office accounting or staffing systems. They only care that there is someone available to answer their questions. In our case, let's say there is an accounting requirement. The copy of the master calendar could be printed out each month and filed. As such, the printout would be called business value-added work; it is necessary, but not in the eyes of the customer.

What if there is no accounting requirement? Then the form has no added value. It does not contribute to customer satisfaction and it does not add value to the business function. The use of the form—the copying, the handling, the signing, the storing—is non–value-added work. The form increases complexity and reduces the productivity of the IR office, so it should be eliminated.

Numerous tools associated with value analysis have been developed. The flowchart is the first and most important. By drawing a visual map of a process, we can clearly see redundant work. To develop a comprehensive flowchart, good interviewing and observation skills are helpful because you need to either listen to people describe their work or watch them do it. Cost buildup charts, which depict the sequence of process activities and the time and cost associated with each activity, are also used in value analysis. The value test is applied to each activity to reduce both the time and costs associated with delivering a customer-satisfying product or service.

Value analysis and a focus on squeezing out unnecessary work are occurring on some campuses across the nation as faculty members, staff members, and administrators respond to the need to do more with less. At the University of California at Santa Cruz (UCSC), for example, business managers in the various colleges reacted to a weak, inflexible financial information system used on campus by developing their own shadow systems. Each business manager moved toward his or her own customized system, adding hardware and software. Then the managers hired extra people to run the increasingly sophisticated, but increasingly redundant, systems. Everyone was trying to do the right thing, but the overall effect was disastrous, as the level of complexity increased at seemingly geometric rates. UCSC is now working hard, using quality management and reengineering principles, to redesign a simple, robust approach that will eliminate the redundancies in the financial information system and increase productivity.

The graduate school at the University of Wisconsin—Madison calculated overall GPAs for applicants to their 128 departments.[5] Calculating the cumulative GPAs, which often spanned many years at many different schools with different grading systems, was tremendously time-consuming work. Why did the graduate school do it? Because the departments wanted it done. Why? According to the departments, they needed cumulative GPAs because the graduate school's fellowship office required them. Since the departments did not know in advance which students they would nominate for fellowships, they needed the numbers for everyone. Why did the fellowship office require cumulative GPAs? Because, according to the fellowship office, the numbers had already been calculated for all applicants as part of the admissions process, so why not use them? Did anyone really need the numbers? No. Poor communication in a fragmented process allowed unnecessary work to seep in. The graduate school, working with the departments, has since reversed the initial two steps in the process (applications go to the departments first, then to the graduate school). By doing so, the departments are able to reduce the annual pool of applicants (using other criteria such as undergraduate major) by more than 5,000. That, in turn, translates into 5,000 fewer GPA calculations each year.

At Pennsylvania State University, the Smeal College of Business Administration provides advising services for thousands of students each semester. After surveying its students, a small team from the Academic Advising Center reached the conclusion that "Customer service could be improved by streamlining the intake and reception process and removing unnecessary steps." The team first made a flowchart of the process, so that all team members could reach consensus and clearly understand how the reception and intake process currently worked. Agreeing that indeed there were unnecessary steps in the process, team members then set out to discover the root causes of the problem. These included:

- Physical setting—Due to lack of space, advising was spread out over three different offices on three different floors.
- Intake form—The form, developed by the faculty without consulting staff, was not being used as intended. Students found it too complex and confusing.
- Intake method—There was no standardized methodology. Processes and procedures had not been designed; they had just evolved.

After benchmarking the reception and intake procedures of five other organizations—focusing particularly on matters pertaining to policy statements, forms, scheduling techniques, and traffic flow—the team was ready to start the redesign. With simplification as their goal, team members squeezed out bureaucratic nonsense, eliminated redundancies, and reorganized their work space. What had been a three-page flowchart filled with loops and wait symbols became a simple, straightforward one-pager. What had been a nightmare of complexity became a slimmed-down process that is getting rave reviews from students and staff alike.

Perhaps the best way to think of complexity is as a thief in the night. Whether it appears as redundant business systems, unnecessary calculations, or a "Request for Vacation or Absence from Office" form, complexity robs you of time and energy. It steals institutional resources and wastes them on meaningless, superfluous tasks. Because of complexity, you have fewer resources for those activities that will truly add value to your work and satisfaction to your work life. The thief is always around, lurking in the shadows, waiting for you to relax. Don't let it happen. Be vigilant. Guard your ways—your simple ways.

QUESTIONS

Map the processes within which you work. Study the steps in terms of time and money.

Review your customers' requirements.

Now, what steps in each process add value to your customer? Those that do not increase the quality of the service to the end user are candidates for elimination.

How can you ensure that simplicity remains a priority?

PART 3

FEEDBACK

PERFORMANCE IMPROVEMENT FRAMEWORK

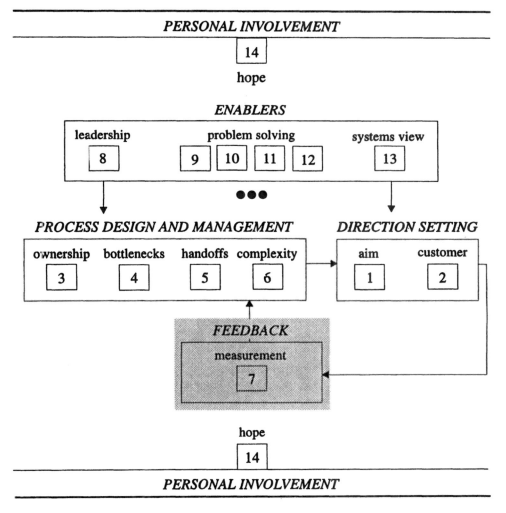

PERSONAL INVOLVEMENT

14

hope

ENABLERS

leadership
8

problem solving
9 10 11 12

systems view
13

PROCESS DESIGN AND MANAGEMENT

ownership bottlenecks handoffs complexity
3   4   5   6

DIRECTION SETTING

aim customer
1   2

FEEDBACK

measurement
7

hope

14

PERSONAL INVOLVEMENT

LESSON 7

"Measurement without feedback is just data; feedback without measurement is just opinion."

Helen worked in the information booth at the front gate of the college four days a week, Thursday through Sunday. She and her husband were both retired and lived across the street from the small school, halfway between New York and Boston on the Rhode Island coast.

Helen didn't need to work, but she enjoyed meeting people and the information booth was great for that. She also enjoyed keeping track of things: organizing, counting, making lists. The information booth wasn't so great for that. She just answered questions, gave directions, and issued parking permits.

One day Helen decided to have some fun. She got an old notebook out and drew some lines—rows and columns. Every time someone wanted a permit or asked a question she made a check. Before long, Helen, sitting in her information booth at the front gate, could tell you a lot about the school. What was the most difficult building to find? Math-Science, definitely. What was the most commonly asked question? A two-part answer: during the week it was, "Do I need a parking permit?" and on the weekends it was, "Is there a campus tour that we could go on?"

❖

Harry, the new vice president for enrollment management, had been on the job for six months. Previously, he had been director of admissions at another college. The new position and the title reflected a sign of the times: competition for qualified college applicants was intense. Competition for applicants wasn't simply a matter of pride or prestige; it was a matter of economic survival. Without a strong first-year class, tuition income would decline, forcing the small college to dip into its reserves.

So here it was, Sunday afternoon, and Harry and his staff were in a New Jersey motel putting the final touches on their week-long blitz of high schools and college fairs in New Jersey and eastern Pennsylvania.

Harry reflected on one of his new initiatives. He was very concerned about the shrinking pool of applications. His "new and improved" campus tour should help. The beauty of the campus, condition of the classrooms, modern dormitories, and state-of-the-art computer labs were major selling points. He had recruited the most enthusiastic students to be tour guides and had personally scripted the tour, drilling the guides on important facts, most-asked questions, and points of interests. Then he sat down with his staff and made up the schedule—every morning at 10:00 and every afternoon at 2:00, Monday through Friday. So far, the results were a bit disappointing. Interest in the tour was not as high as he had hoped.

❖

Sue would be a senior this coming year. She was looking forward to her final year in high school and then going on to college. She wanted to attend a small school, not too far from her home in New York, like the one only a few miles from the family's summer house on the Rhode Island shore.

In fact, this weekend Sue and her family had decided to stop at the school on their way back to New York. Pulling into the college's entrance, Sue's mom spotted the information booth. The car came to a halt next to it and Sue popped *out of the back seat. A kindly, older woman greeted her with a smile and said, "Hello, how can I help you?"*

Sue replied, "Is there a campus tour we could go on?"

"No, I'm so sorry," said the woman. "Campus tours are conducted at 10:00 A.M. and 2:00 P.M. Monday through Friday."

As Sue and her parents drove back to New York, they talked about the college in Connecticut they had visited last weekend.

As Sue and her parents drove back to New York, Harry's motel meeting was in full swing.

As Sue and her parents drove back to New York, Helen made another check.

❖❖❖

The word *improve* means to make or become better. In our society, some of this meaning has been lost in the daily hype of commercialism; everything is "new and improved." If it isn't new and improved now, wait a week and it will be. Put little green crystals in a box of soap, add a drop of propylene glycol to hand lotion, and you have the makings of a reinvigorated marketing campaign.

In spite of the ubiquitous use of the terminology *new and improved,* there is a much more rigorous way to think about becoming better. The PDCA cycle (plan, do, check, and act) is a methodology for learning and improvement. Developed by Walter Shewhart in the 1930s and made popular by W. Edwards Deming (the Deming wheel), it is presented as a series of activities. Plan improvements in current practices. Put the plan into action, and check to see whether carrying out the plan yields the desired improvement. Act to prevent recurrence of the old ways and to institutionalize the improvement as a new practice to improve upon. The presumption is that as you proceed through the cycle, individuals and organizations *continuously* improve their performance.[1]

Having a methodology for improvement is critical. Too often the notion of new and improved has been the fantasy of marketers. If you couple the rhetoric of improvement with that of quality, the result is frequently sheer whimsy and illusion. What exactly does a statement such as "We need to improve our quality" actually mean? More important, how do you do it? Where do you begin? How do you know whether you are successful? How can you ensure that you will continue to improve? These questions suggest that talking a good quality game is not enough. There must be a rigorous framework for performance improvement.

PDCA cycle thinking is a more than adequate start. It replaces the mythology of improvement with a methodology for improvement. New standards are set only to be challenged, revised, and replaced by newer and better standards. Having a methodology moves us from the realm of wishful thinking to the reality of having a process to actually make improvements. By connecting a series of daily organizational activities into an iterative process, PDCA thinking creates a mechanism and force for change. It creates a deep learning cycle that enables individuals and institutions to stretch and grow. Without such close connections, energy is dissipated, good ideas are lost, and carefully crafted visions remain unfulfilled. In the end, things tend to remain pretty much the same as they have always been.

The lesson of Helen, Harry, and Sue deals with two of the major disconnects between methodology and mythology that keep our colleges and universities from changing and improving. The first is reflected in the phrase "Measurement without feedback is just data." It would be impossible to overstate the importance of measurement in process improvement. Performance measures are the "vital signs" of an organization. They help us to understand what is occurring, reveal the need for change, demonstrate the impact of change, and determine priorities. The quality literature, in particular, is packed full of wise epigrams on measurement, such as, "If you can't measure it, you can't understand it; if you can't understand it you can't control it; and if you can't control it you can't improve it," "Every process generates the data to improve it," and "What gets measured, gets done."[2]

A key aspect of these sayings is that measurement is never mentioned alone. It always has a sidekick. Like an older brother being shadowed by a kid brother, successful measurement is always closely followed by another action, an adjustment or change. A feedback loop communicates knowledge of results. This tight connection between measurement and feedback is evidenced in the PDCA cycle.[3] Immediately following the execution or *do* stage of the cycle is a *check* stage, a data-gathering or performance measurement step that monitors progress toward the plan. A study of the results of a plan informs the next stage in the cycle, the *act* stage. The act stage might consist of formalizing those actions that were successful or making changes to the plan in those areas where expectations were not met. In effect, performance measures are gathered so that we are able to compare the *do* against the *plan*. By asking "What did we learn?" we can decide whether to adopt the change or abandon it. This is how a reflective practitioner operates on a daily basis—always questioning the effect that an action creates.

Unfortunately, PDCA thinking does not often occur on a college campus. The story that opens the chapter is illustrative. Harry had a plan. He scripted, he drilled, and he scheduled. Then he unleashed his "new and improved" campus tour. Harry's almost nonexistent check stage includes one piece of data that could be used to inform change: he knows that fewer prospective students are taking the tour than expected. That information falls far short of the kind of performance measures he needs to make anything other than an uneducated guess as to what to do next.

Helen, in contrast, has data that would be of great value. If anyone asked her, she could explain that, because of the school's location, the weekends produce a steady stream of campus visitors. Her tally sheets tell the story in a series of check marks. Because there is no feedback loop, however, her marks remain raw scratches on a piece of paper, not information that can be used to reduce uncertainty in decision making. And that is the key. Measurement that cannot be used to inform choices is just data—columns and rows of numbers with no connection to further action. As important as measurement is, by itself it is worthless.

Most college campuses are awash in data but thirsty for information. The data come in all shapes and sizes, and from a variety of sources for a range of purposes. Some of the data are the kind that Helen is collecting—potentially useful but not organized and disseminated in a way to yield timely feedback. Other data are gathered for the purpose of evaluating specific management issues. When conditions change, however, the performance measurement system often does not. The result is a series of ritualistic exercises in which data are collected, analyzed, and reported in studies and memos, providing detailed answers to questions that no one is asking anymore. (See, for example, the story that introduces lesson 9, "To create the future, challenge the past.") Then there are the "because we asked for it" data that are collected for the narrow purposes of accountability and control. Few of these data are connected with the day-to-day challenge of improving performance on a college campus. Indeed, most of the data are accumulated by state education officials and boards eager to compare institutions in an ever-vigilant search for laggards and by accrediting agencies charged with the responsibility of enforcing minimum standards.

In all these instances the data flow is one-way. In contrast, performance measures that yield information (not data) on the effectiveness and efficiency of a process do so because the measures enable the decision maker to tie means more closely to ends, causes to effects. With such tight loops, "vital signs" can be used by individuals to inform action, reduce uncertainty, and continuously improve performance.

One of the best illustrations of tight feedback connections that drive performance improvement is in the student assessment movement. K. Patricia Cross, one of assessment's most articulate advocates, has been working to link assessment with classroom activities and student learning. PDCA thinking is evident in her words: "The purpose of classroom assessment is to maximize learning through frequent assessments of how well students are meeting the goals of instruction [comparing the *check* against the *plan*]." She goes on to add, "Classroom assessment procedures involve collecting data from students periodically throughout the term or semester [check] and then using that information to modify teaching [act], constantly experimenting [plan] to see how teachers can be more effective in maximizing learning [do]."[4] This notion of assessment as information is built on the feedback principle. Student learning can be significantly improved if the learners have an appropriate knowledge of results that shows them how much progress they have made and points out specific areas where additional work is needed.

Properly conceived and administered academic programs also rely on strong measurement-feedback loops. At Central Missouri State University, for example, the nursing program has developed a "continuous process assessment plan." The plan seeks to generate performance measures on various aspects of the nursing program involving alumni, students, and faculty members. Further, a six-part evaluation process (consisting of assessor, assessment process, coordinator, assessment time frame, recipient of assessment information, and impact on development and revision of the program) provides a framework for improvement based on linking performance measurement and feedback.

For example, the alumni component of the plan has four different assessors: self, employer, NCLEX-RN (licensure exam), and the nursing program's advisory board. The alumni self-assessment component is as follows:

- Assessment process: Questionnaires are sent to alumni at one and three years post graduation. Data are generated regarding satisfaction with program's preparation, assessment of self relative to outcomes, and patterns of employment and service.
- Coordinator of assessment: Continuous Process Assessment Committee (CPAC).
- Assessment time frame: Sent out in Spring.
- Recipient of assessment data: Faculty via CPAC annual committee report.

- Impact on development and revision of program: To curriculum committee for consideration in curriculum revision.

The employer assessor of the alumni component differs from self-assessment in two areas:

- Assessment process: Questionnaires are sent to employers of alumni. Data are gathered regarding their assessment of program and of alumni.
- Impact on development and revision of program: To RN Advanced Placement Committee for recruitment efforts and/or program revision.

Measurement without feedback is, indeed, just data and has little ability to effect purposeful change. Without a measurement-feedback loop, improvement is haphazard at best, nonexistent at worst. Maintenance of the status quo or degradation—a slow and steady decline in performance—are the only real possibilities. In contrast, the examples of successful student and program assessment efforts illustrate how indispensable the measurement-feedback link is to any effort that has comprehensive and continuous improvement as its goal.

A second disconnection we experience in our efforts to improve quality and productivity in higher education is evidenced in the other half of the lesson—"feedback without measurement is just opinion." As I have noted, in the last decade there has been an explosion of data—and institutional research personnel—to feed the ravenous appetite of external agencies and education bureaucracies. Only a few scraps of such data, however, have found their way into the daily activities of faculty members, administrators, and staff. Many campus meetings, instead, are characterized by a pat routine: a problem is noted, opinions are voiced, anecdotes are shared, and a decision is made. The driving force of the meeting is to make the problem go away—information or no information.

There is plenty of feedback during one of these meetings. Everyone can tell a story from his or her own personal experience and then extend an opinion on how things ought to be. The plural of *anecdote* is not *information*, however, and a roomful of opinions does not constitute management-by-fact.

The same two units of analysis used to illustrate that "measurement without feedback is just data"—that is, the student and an academic program—can also be used to illustrate that "feedback without measurement is just opinion." First, the student. Student assessment and classroom research efforts can provide feedback that reflects a knowledge of results. Such feedback enables the student and professor to plan what to do next. But how much of this type of feedback actually occurs with students? Regretfully, performance-enhancing feedback in the student arena is the exception. The rule is something quite different. A recent article by John B. Bennett and Elizabeth A. Dreyer begins:

> Faculty complaining about students' deficiencies has become a cottage industry. No institutional type or sector of higher education seems spared. Each fall, last year's grim stories are updated and enhanced in offices and lounges and at national meetings. Students' historical, geographical, linguistic, and scientific ignorance is outlined; their underdeveloped communication skills are remarked; and their passivity in their own learning lamented.[5]

It's sad but true. Few professors engage in a rigorous approach to student learning that marries performance measures with feedback. The only performance measures many professors give are mid-term and final grades; the only performance measures they get are student course evaluations. Such measures are not designed to improve performance but rather to rank and sort (students for grades, faculty members for promotion and tenure). Feedback on student performance tends to get trivialized and sidetracked to faculty lounges, precisely as Bennett and Dreyer describe. Moreover, as they go on to comment, such complaining and storytelling are problematic when they serve to shield the complainer, when problems are projected and assigned elsewhere, or when faults are presented as always occurring in learning, never in teaching. In spite of all the storytelling and opinion making, therefore, the quality and rate of student learning are unimproved.

At the academic program level, I can use an illustration from another Missouri state school—Northwest Missouri State University (NW). Several years ago, the president of NW, Dean Hubbard, watched while another president distributed a report in the budget committee of the state legislature outlining the first-time pass rates of students on the CPA exam. Of course, the students from the institution whose president chose to distribute the report topped the list. President Hubbard's institution came in last. Upon his return to campus, the president called a meeting where he asked the dean and the chair of accounting, "What do you make of this?" The chair, since retired, went through a somewhat predictable process. First he denied that the report was true. Then he said the problem was one of resources; other schools offered more accounting courses than NW. Finally, he asserted the report's authors were measuring the wrong thing. Accounting firms, the chair argued, really wanted students who could communicate well and the other institutions were too technical. The president's response was, "How do you know that?"

At the end of the meeting, President Hubbard stated, "All I'm asking is that you develop a strategy to understand clearly and precisely what your customers—in this case the people that hire our graduates—want." A new accounting professor responded to the challenge. She studied other schools (interestingly, the top school in the state required two fewer courses in accounting), conducted focus groups with employers, surveyed past graduates, and used the information she gathered to suggest improvements in the content and sequencing of course work. Today, Northwest's accounting students are at the top in the state, by a country mile.

I began this lesson by suggesting that performance improvement does not just happen. We must make improvements happen, so why don't we? The principle problem is not with the lack of data. We have plenty of data. Ask any institutional researcher; most have difficulty sleeping at night, what with the sound of crunching numbers in their heads. Or ask Helen. She has a notepad full of chicken scratches. We also have plenty of feedback. Ask any professor or administrator. Each can instantly recall a good, juicy story. Or ask Harry. His staff members will be more than happy to provide their opinions. What we do not have—and what we so desperately need if we are to improve the quality and productivity of our institutions—are compelling aims, strong performance measures, and tight feedback loops. We don't have a methodology for learning and improving that connects direction setting with process, design, and management.

If we did, Harry might not be working out of a motel in New Jersey, while prospective students, like Sue, are being turned away at the campus gate in Rhode Island.

QUESTIONS

For any process the following questions should be asked and answered:

Why should we measure? Where should we measure? What should we measure? When should we measure? Who should do the measuring?

Also, why should we provide feedback? What feedback should we provide? To whom should we provide it? When should we provide it? Who should provide it?

PART 4

ENABLERS

PERFORMANCE IMPROVEMENT FRAMEWORK

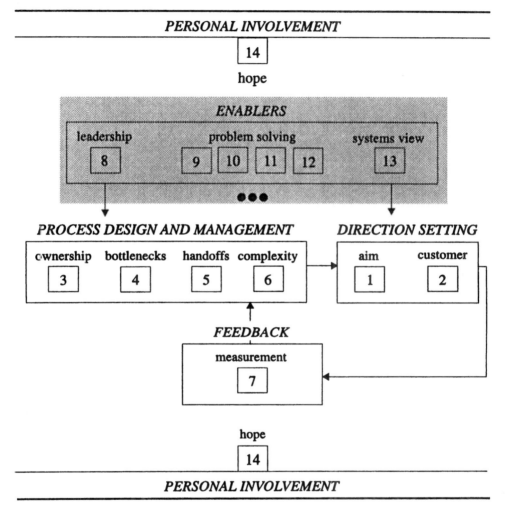

PERSONAL INVOLVEMENT

14

hope

ENABLERS

leadership   problem solving   systems view

8   9   10   11   12   13

● ● ●

PROCESS DESIGN AND MANAGEMENT   *DIRECTION SETTING*

ownership   bottlenecks   handoffs   complexity   aim   customer

3   4   5   6   1   2

FEEDBACK

measurement

7

hope

14

PERSONAL INVOLVEMENT

LESSON 8

"Followers, not leaders, are the best judges of hypocrisy."

Monday morning. Dana Maxfield, director of campus safety, made two sharp lefts and pulled into a parking space. He stepped out into the warm, early morning sun. After a week in Michigan, where they had more snowblowers than southern California had palm trees, he was glad to be back home. Two minutes later he was sitting in his office.

Dana had just begun to empty his briefcase of the hand-outs and notes from the conference he had attended when his secretary, Jaci, blew into his office.

"This was sent out last week," she said, waving something in the air. "It's disgusting. Everyone got one. Courtney in the physical plant said that some people down there wanted to do something—you know, get a petition going or some-thing." Dana tried to calm her down, but she had had the entire weekend to build up steam and she was not about to let anyone stop her from venting. He finally managed to snatch the papers out of midair as they made a pass in front of his face. Jaci kept talking. He read.

The top of the front page had the university logo. Beneath it, in bold letters, was "Cumulative Absenteeism and Tardi-ness Policy." A small box to the right had "Policy #" printed in it, followed by a typed "337." Dana glanced down the page. The policy began, "1.0 PURPOSE: Absenteeism, whether excused or unexcused, causes undue hardship on coworkers. For this reason absenteeism must be controlled by adhering to the Absenteeism and Tardiness Policy. Accordingly, cumulative absence and tardiness, excused or unexcused, will be dealt with based on an absence point system."

Dana flipped through the pages. There were seven. One page was filled with detailed definitions of "tardiness" and "absence." On another page the point system was explained: an absence was 1 point, tardiness .5 point. The policy continued, "3–3.5 points within a year will warrant an informal counseling; 5–5.5 points a written counseling; 7–7.5 progressive suspension; 9 or more points suspension with intent to terminate." The last two pages contained examples, all ending in termination.

Dana was having trouble comprehending the whole thing. Sure, he had a few people who tended to show up 5 or 10 minutes late, and he had finally talked to them. One, an officer, had been "like a clock" ever since. The other, a secretary, transferred to another department on campus. But a seven-page policy?

❖

On Tuesday, just as Dana and several of his officers were about to leave the cafeteria, in walked Ray Scarpa, the associate vice president for human resources. It was Ray's signature that adorned page seven of policy #337.

Dana didn't know Ray that well. They both reported to the vice president for administration, Maria Marquez, but most of the interaction between their offices was routine. The only time he really saw Ray was every other Tuesday at the quality council meetings. Maria had formed the council almost a year ago. The idea was to find ways to improve the efficiency and effectiveness of the services in the division. An outside consultant had been working with the group, doing training on topics such as vision setting, teamwork, using statistical tools, and so on.

Dana caught Ray's eye, skirted a few tables, and managed to catch him before he sat down. "I was wondering if I could come over and see you some time this week."

"Sure, I think Friday afternoon's pretty open. Why? What's up?"

"That policy, the one on absenteeism, is causing me some trouble. I was wondering if . . ." Ray never let him finish. He spit out, "Everybody knows it's lax around here. People just come and go as they please." Dana started to say, "Well, I know some people . . ." Cut off again. "It's not just some people. It's a good policy and we needed one."

Dana decided to retreat in the face of overwhelming odds. "Well, let me look it over and I'll talk to you later—maybe at the meeting next week."

❖

Wednesday morning the paving trucks and equipment were out in force. Within the confines of yards of yellow tape, the crew was busy repaving and relining the parking lot. Dana made a right at the intersection and headed toward lot 12. It was still early, before 8:00 A.M., so he could probably find a space there. Why hadn't someone told him about this?

It was almost 9:00 when Jaci and Niki, Jaci's car-pool buddy, came bustling into the office. "What's with the yellow tape all over campus? We had to park over by the gym," Jaci announced. Niki looked down at her feet and added, "A 20-minute walk in heels."

Adrian, the desk officer, looked over at Dana, "Points. This is going to cost you, ladies. I didn't see any high heel waivers in the policy."

As Dana returned to his office, several other people joined the fray. The last thing he heard before shutting his door was Niki saying, "It's stupid. It's humiliating and stupid." And it was, thought Dana. There were 15 people meeting every other week to talk about empowerment, teamwork, and *plans to improve productivity. In fact, Maria and Ray had decided two weeks ago to pilot two projects, one in the physical plant and the other in campus safety. He needed to identify a problem, generate a team of people, and start training them next week. How could he do that? Who would volunteer?*

Dana picked up the phone and called Maria's office.

❖

Late in the afternoon on Thursday, Dana began by telling Maria about the problems the new policy was causing in his office. He then jumped to the pilot project, explaining that, as it stood right now, no one was in the mood to volunteer for anything. They were angry. She listened. Then she stood and said, "We knew there would be some problems with the policy, but we also knew that things were too lax. We needed to tighten up."

Walking around to the other side of the desk, Maria continued, "What I don't understand is what this has to do with the pilot project. The quality council meets on Tuesday. The absenteeism policy was drafted by my staff. They meet on Monday."

❖❖❖

You are part of a small band foraging for food, but it is winter and food is becoming scarce. A river to the south runs fast and deep. On the other side, the land looks rich and game plentiful. The only passage, however, is a long, narrow log. Do you stay and hope that spring will come soon, or do you risk the raging waters?

Organizations face the log dilemma every day. As their environment shifts—markets disappear, competition increases, technology obsolesces—they must consider dramatically different ways of conducting their business. Higher education is no exception. Colleges and universities face mounting concerns over access, costs, and the quality and productivity of teaching and learning. They can hunker down and hope for an early thaw, or they can choose to explore different ways of managing the academic enterprise. (See also the next lesson, "To create the future, challenge the past.")

A significant factor that influences the decision of our forager, our business person, and our college educator is the nature of leadership. Change is scary. In most cases, it is easier to sit tight, hope for a business uptick, or believe in the inevitability of cycles rather than risk harm or injury. There is comfort in the known, discomfort in the unknown.

Enter the leader. A leader, according to the futurist Joel Barker, is "a person you will follow to a place you wouldn't go yourself."[1] A narrow log over a raging river qualifies as a place you wouldn't go. Abandoning an increasingly ineffective but familiar technology for a new, untested technology is a place you probably wouldn't want to go. Shifting from a traditional notion of excellence in education that relies on resources and reputation to an educational paradigm that stresses value-added performance is another place you probably wouldn't want to go.

In all cases, followers scrutinize the words and actions of leaders. Followers want to be reassured that tomorrow will be better than today, that where they are going offers more opportunity than where they are now. They need to be convinced that their current position is untenable and that the risks associated with change are acceptable. They listen intently to hear the right words, spoken with clarity and honesty. They watch carefully to see that beliefs are manifested in strong, purposeful actions, that what leaders say matches what they do.

What type of person can stand up to this kind of scrutiny? Steven Covey, in his work on principle-centered leadership, makes a distinction between people who operate inside-out versus those who operate outside-in.[2] He suggests that if we want to develop the trust that results in lasting solutions, we must start first with "the self." An inside-out approach is based on the idea that private victories precede public victories. Making and keeping promises to ourselves precede making and keeping promises to others. The inside-out approach is a continuing process of self-renewal:

> So if you want to *have* a happy marriage, *be* the kind of person who generates positive energy and sidesteps negative energy. If you want to *have* a more pleasant, cooperative teenager, *be* a more understanding, empathetic, consistent, loving parent. If you want to *have* more freedom, more latitude in your job, *be* a more responsible, helpful, contributing employee. If you want to be trusted, be trustworthy.[3]

Applying the inside-out approach to our log dilemma is relatively straightforward. True leaders—those who can inspire others to risk going places they wouldn't go themselves—search their own conscience for truth and understanding. They reconcile danger with hope and seek to conquer their own fears. They believe in themselves, in their ability to develop the capacity to follow in others, and in the rightness of the chosen course of action. Then, and only then, do they step resolutely onto the log with a strong personal conviction that they can make a difference.

There are a number of such leaders in higher education. A leadership team that comes to mind is at Samford University, a 4,000-student Baptist institution, located in Birmingham, Alabama. President Tom Corts, William Hull, the provost, and his assistant, John Harris, are a formidable corps of inside-out leaders who are committed to applying the principles of quality management to both the administrative and academic sides of their university. The key to this statement is the word *committed*. It is one thing to commit others to something; it is quite different to commit yourself. The individuals at Samford have not bought an off-the-shelf set of ideas and designated a group of underlings to sell it to the campus community. There is nothing superficial or fleeting about their commitment; it comes from deep within themselves.

Illustrations of this commitment can be found in William Hull's "Occasional Papers of the Provost," a collection of personal musings that he shares with the campus community. Given the institution's religious affiliation and Hull's own background as a religion professor, the papers often reflect a thoughtful blending of new management approaches and spiritual inquiry. For example, in one paper Hull reflects on quality concepts and religious teachings: "An essential characteristic of quality is conformity to expectations, what prophet Amos called being judged by a plumb line that does not deceive (Amos 7:7–9)." In another section, while quoting from John (4:38), he talks about the interdependent nature of quality and the importance of forming partnerships.

The commitment that Samford's leaders have made is deeply personal. It should, therefore, come as no surprise that the Samford University community—faculty members, staff, administrators, and students—has achieved significant performance gains across a broad spectrum of work activities. Test scores have increased, costs have decreased, and morale has climbed. Public victories have, indeed, followed from the private victories of Samford's leaders.

Another example of inside-out leadership comes from Belmont University in Nashville, Tennessee. William Troutt is Belmont's president, and Susan Hillenmeyer is one of the institution's vice presidents. Together, with a great deal of help from an involved and inspired campus community, they have begun to re-create the university as a true learning organization. Much of the community's willingness to engage itself in an institutional renewal process can be traced to the willingness of leaders to involve themselves in individual change processes. In the summer of 1993, for example, Belmont's board of trustees rewarded president Troutt for 10 years of service by providing him with a study leave. He spent the time traveling the country, speaking with leaders of such highly successful organizations as Harley-Davidson, Proctor & Gamble, and Ritz-Carlton.

In an issue of Belmont's alumni magazine, Troutt discussed his findings. Truly gifted leaders, he found, influence change and growth in a variety of ways, yet their organizations share a set of common features: a big long-term shared vision; a relentless focus on what they believe in; a balanced approach to whom they serve; a simply stated, meaningful mission that everyone understands; a set of public measures of performance; a focus on candid conversation and honest relationships; and a commitment to continued learning. He closed by saying, "Belmont may be one of the few universities in the country that possesses the people, the will and the bedrock values to rise to be this type of organization. We have a way to go, but we are improving and learning about ourselves as fast as any college or university I know."

Harry Forsha, in his book *The Pursuit of Quality through Personal Change*, addresses directly the challenge of leadership in promoting the type of organizational transformation underway at Samford and Belmont. He says, "If *you* want to change something, then the action must come from *you*." Without such a personal commitment, the words of leaders are viewed as pure and simple hypocrisy. The words have no meaning. They are like soap bubbles, pretty to look at as they rise up, float away on the wind, and eventually disappear without a trace. Forsha continues, "To do otherwise is to remove yourself from the process. To remove yourself from the process may very well eliminate any hope you have of influencing the results."[4]

Our story is a singular illustration of this recurring theme. Maria, the vice president for administration, committed her portion of the organization to a quality improvement effort. She brought in a consultant, did training, appointed a council, and scheduled meetings. She spent money, developed an infrastructure, and invested her time and the time of her subordinates. In a conventional sense, she is committed, yet something is painfully wrong.

Maria's actions—the issuance of a dehumanizing, fear-invoking absenteeism and tardiness policy—stand in sharp contrast to the principles that were undoubtedly espoused in the training. In effect, her approach to change is outside-in. She is convinced that the problem is "out there." Her workers need to shape up or ship out. They need to work smarter and harder, so she schedules training and meetings and develops strict policies on attendance.

Chances are, Maria has all the rhetoric down pat. She can quote Deming, recite his 14 points, and discuss his seven deadly sins. Her hallway conversations are probably spiced with words such as *customer* and *vision*. Pretty soon she will be able to brag about how many of her people have been trained in TQM.

But what will change? The answer is nothing. Maria, by removing herself from the process, has doomed any and all efforts to improve the performance of her organization. That's because the change was never about her, always about them. The seven-page policy tipped her hand; it's the same old Maria. She's a hypocrite and her followers know it. The money that she has thrown at training is wasted; the time devoted to future meetings and projects is largely wasted, too. Change is dead. No one will trust her and no will follow her—not onto a log, not anywhere that they would not go.

QUESTIONS

Review your own calendar and meeting agendas. Look through recent speeches. Has your behavior changed to reflect your rhetoric?

Most performance evaluation is top-down. If you were to develop a bottom-up evaluation to improve your own performance, what questions would you ask of people who report to you? How would you use that feedback to improve your own performance?

LESSON 9

"To create the future, challenge the past."

He came in the winter. She came at least once a week. He was the new district vice president for academic affairs. She was a secretary, one of several assigned to the office, who would stop to ask whether any noncredit teaching sheets had arrived from any of the colleges. Each sheet showed the title of the class, the person who was teaching it, the number of students enrolled, how much was being charged per student, how much the instructor was being paid, and several other items.

By the time summer rolled around, she had an 18-inch stack of sheets on her desk. Through the hot months of June and July, she labored over the small mountain of data—adding items together, rearranging columns, and alphabetizing everything in sight.

One day in early August she walked into his office and proudly announced, "Here it is." She waved "it" back and forth, smiled brightly, and placed it squarely in the middle of his desk.

The now-not-so-new vice president said, "What's this?" She explained it was a comprehensive analysis of noncredit classes taught at the colleges during the past year.

He said, "Why do you do the report?" She said, "I've been doing it for the past 10 years."

He said, "To whom do I give the report?" She said, "It's for you."

He said, "What do I do with the report?" She said, "It goes in the file cabinet, over there, with the others."

❖❖❖

The list of critical issues our colleges and universities face is daunting. Concerns about increasing accountability, spiraling tuitions, and flat or declining budgets are tattooed on our collective psyche. If that is not enough to think about, we can always reflect on the 1993 report of the Wingspread Group on Higher Education, *An American Imperative*, which was noted in the preface. The opening quote of the report, again: "A disturbing and dangerous mismatch exists between what American society needs of higher education and what it is receiving." The report continues, "Nowhere is the mismatch more dangerous than in the quality of the undergraduate preparation provided on many campuses. The American imperative for the 21st century is that society must hold higher education to much higher expectations or risk national decline."[1]

Given this environment—one that seems to be crying out for new and different ideas—it is not surprising that when the Pew Collaborative (a meeting, sponsored by the Pew Charitable Trusts, of colleges and universities committed to restructuring) announced its November 1993 inaugural meeting, intended to "build a common base for restructuring," 450 institutional leaders showed up and another 250 were turned away for lack of space. When it comes to transformation, we are in the midst of an inclusion frenzy. Just mention the necessary syllable "re"—as in rethinking visions, reinventing learning, reengineering processes, or redesigning curricula—and a crowd of educators is likely to gather.

Before we get too far down this transformation highway, however, we need to apply the brakes and consider the rhetoric of change espoused in a gathering of institutional leaders versus the reality of change practiced on a college campus. Our opening story is a useful starting point. Is it an extreme example? Do things like this occur on a college campus? Do individuals really labor for months on a document without questioning the relevance of their work? Of course they do. Most situations are not quite so flagrant. Instead, they usually involve more subtle scenarios that are played out each day in department offices, in admissions, financial aid, or in the library. Other times, the stage is set for a larger production, perhaps on a task force or in a series of committee meetings. Presidents' offices and professors' classrooms are not immune from such locked-in thinking patterns either.

The preparation of the report in the story illustrates the kind of deep grooves that permeate organizations. Initial assumptions are made. Habits and ingrained routines based upon those assumptions become accepted practices, "the way we do things around here." The grooves get etched deeper and deeper. Thinking patterns crystallize, stabilize, and then calcify. Regardless of the situation or changes in circumstances, old programming begins to dictate everything: what questions are asked, what information is gathered, what options are considered. Renewal under such conditions is a battle that is often not worth waging.

The literature in organizational behavior, industrial psychology, social psychology, and other areas is replete with studies and reports on the dynamics of change. Researchers and writers have engaged in detailed analyses of virtually every aspect of the subject. Still, the most basic truth that has emerged from this concentrated inquiry is that unchallenged assumptions are the bane of any effort to budge the status quo.

Let me give you just a small sampling of the sheer breadth and depth of this axiom. In the scientific world, Thomas Kuhn wrote about the concept of the paradigm in *The Structure of Scientific Revolutions*.[2] A paradigm is a framework of thought that is shared and accepted. Because a paradigm defines boundaries and details acceptable practices inside those boundaries, it is a powerful concept. A paradigm is quite useful in a scientific setting because it brings coherency to scientific research—

useful, that is, until fewer and fewer problems can be solved within the old paradigm and a new one must emerge. It is at this point, the paradigm shift, that difficulties develop. Many people, according to Kuhn, are unwilling or unable to think beyond the paradigm within which they have long operated, even when the rules of that paradigm no longer work. That is because a paradigm, by its very definition, determines what we see *and what we don't see.*

Joel Barker has helped to make *paradigm* a common term by suggesting that what Kuhn discovered in science holds for the human condition. Barker's principal paradigm shift question is, What is impossible to do in your field, but, if it could be done, would fundamentally change it? A "fundamental change" is, in effect, a paradigm shift. Further, he suggests that the only way to achieve such change is to think the impossible, that is, to question the assumptions implicit within your own operating boundaries.

Two other unlikely experts, a nineteenth-century psychologist and today's leading authority on creative thinking, share this belief. Kurt Lewin, the leading advocate of experiential learning in his day, suggested that in order for learning to take place, an individual had to first "unfreeze" him- or herself from present beliefs. Edward de Bono takes a similar tack when he tries to develop in people a sense of "creative dissatisfaction" such that they recognize the current way for what it is—the current way, not necessarily the best way.

Still further, in the emerging field of organizational learning, such individuals as Peter Senge, David Garvin, Chris Argyris, and Daniel Kim have argued that most organizations have shared assumptions that protect the status quo and provide few opportunities for learning. Standard operating procedures can become so institutionalized that competence becomes associated with how well one adheres to the rules. Therein lies the rub: the wider the range of situations subsumed by the routines and the better the routinized performance, the fewer the reminders there are that something besides routinized competence might on occasion be useful or even essential to survival. Indeed, one expert on the subject of knowledge-creating organizations (those organizations that define their vision in terms of continuous innovation) stated in a recent *Harvard Business Review* article that the key to new knowledge is "continuously challenging employees to reexamine what they take for granted."[3]

Finally, there is the commonsense perspective. The sagacious consultant in *The Goal* voices it when he says to the young plant manager, "Alex, if you're like nearly everybody else in this world, you've accepted so many things without question that you're not really thinking at all."[4] The definition of insanity as stated in the Alcoholics Anonymous Big Book offers the same level-headedness: "Insanity is doing the same thing, the same way, and expecting a different result."

If colleges and universities are serious about transformation, there is an obvious place to begin. Tinkering at the edges is not that place. Reshuffling the boxes on the organizational chart or developing a series of new degree programs is not the place either. Transformation, or re-creating the institution, begins by challenging the sanity of doing things the same way they have always been done. New knowledge and insights in higher education are needed because the old paradigms are insufficient to solve our current quality and productivity problems. The place to begin is to identify, enumerate, and discuss the deep grooves that keep us as institutions from learning and growing. The goal is not change; the goal is renewal. That means replacing or redoing what is not working and retaining and improving what is working.

In an earlier lesson I used the curriculum management process at George Mason University (GMU) to illustrate the concept of a bottleneck. The problem is certainly not unique to GMU. Indeed, given the haphazard way most college curricula have evolved, it would not be much of a stretch to suggest that the overwhelming majority of institutions have major problems in the development and delivery of course work. GMU, however, is unique in another way: it has engaged its stakeholders in dialogue.

Through discussions with stakeholders about why and how the process evolved into its present form, a series of assumptions was revealed. These assumptions are as follows:

- Scheduling is driven by faculty preferences. The first three rounds of course scheduling are rooted in negotiations with faculty. Student demands, which are often not clearly understood, are incorporated late in the process and in some cases not at all. Although faculty members get several months to react to the draft schedules, students get only a few days. Department chairs, deans, the provost, and sometimes even the president are appropriate authorities for faculty to call upon for changes if the published schedules do not meet their preferences.

- Students have no responsibility for the schedules. Their only job is to check with advisors to make sure they are fulfilling requirements and to register for the coming semester during the prescribed registration periods.

- Student Records office controls all the rooms. The office is responsible for finding rooms to meet departmental requests. It must negotiate with various parties for changes when rooms are not available. Few blocks of rooms are assigned to schools for local scheduling.

- There are three patterns for classes. Monday-Wednesday-Friday (MWF) for one hour each; Tuesday-Thursday (TR) for one and one-half hours each; or Monday, Tuesday, Wednesday, or Thursday evening for three hours each. Other patterns, such as Tuesday-Thursday-Saturday (TRS), are taboo.

- The summer schedule is independent of other schedules. Summer budgets and summer full-time-equivalent (FTE) formulas are different from academic-year budgets and FTE formulas.

- Graduate schedules are determined separately from undergraduate schedules.

- The published schedule is a mini-catalog. This format adds to the time needed to compile information.

- Each year's schedule is a variant of last year's.

It would be fruitless—an utter waste of good people's valuable time—to try to increase capacity at the bottleneck described (the unavailability of space in prerequisite and required courses) if these assumptions remain unchallenged. Certainly the number of closed classes could be reduced if there were more money to hire adjuncts for additional sections. Possibly the time-to-graduation might be lessened by improving and expanding advising services, but that is old programming. The gains from such changes would be marginal because the paradigm—the process of course development and delivery should be driven by faculty preferences—remains solidly intact.

To shift this paradigm so that GMU can create a more need-satisfying future for all the stakeholders of the process, faculty and administrators need to challenge the assumptions that drive their current thinking. Challenging assumptions requires dialogue, a sustained collective inquiry into the processes, assumptions, and certainties that comprise everyday experiences.[5] People need to suspend their defensive routines ("that's just the way we do things") and probe the underlying reasons why those routines exist. By doing so, they free themselves to act more effectively. At GMU this means confronting administrators' and professors' assumptions regarding the curriculum management system in an attempt to see things with new eyes.

One place where such reflection is producing exciting paradigm-busting work is at Central Missouri State University (CMSU). In the late 1980s, faculty members and administrators at CMSU began exploring what it meant to say that student learning was the university's mission and primary purpose. The question that kept being revisited was, How do we know whether we are successful? The anxiety surrounding this question became increasingly pronounced as faculty and administrators explored the assessment-as-learning approach pioneered by Alverno College. That approach is a multidimensional process of judging the individual in action on the basis of explicit outcomes. As CMSU faculty and administrators studied and gained an appreciation for the principles underlying an ability-based education model, they began to confront their own assumptions.

The dominant assumption, sitting like a boulder in the middle of a narrow roadway, was the course-credit model. The model says that required courses are the basis for organizing a degree program and individual courses evolve as discrete packages of knowledge. Given this organizing principle, the answer to the question of how to define success is quite simple for most colleges and universities. Success is the ability of a student to accumulate credit for 40 courses and satisfy all the distribution requirements. In effect, if a student graduates, the institution has succeeded.

Central Missouri is hard at work trying to shift the paradigm to one in which explicitly defined performance-based student abilities are the organizing principle for the curriculum. The old paradigm—40 courses—holds time constant while performance varies. The new paradigm reverses the two. Performance becomes the constant: students must be able to demonstrate the required competencies. Time becomes the variable: different people will need different amounts of time to acquire and demonstrate these competencies. Such drastically revised assumptions may be tilting at the windmills of tradition, but the prospects for significant renewal are minimal if the institution and its individuals hold on tightly to yesterday's routines. Vigorous dialogue that seeks to reveal patterned thinking, nurture a healthy discontent with the status quo, and unfreeze stuck beliefs is the methodology for transforming Central Missouri. It is also the approach that is required to improve the quality and productivity at other transformation-minded institutions.

There is a final question that needs to be asked. Most people agree that our colleges and universities would benefit from a paradigm shift or two. Further, I have shown that successful renewal requires the willingness and ability to challenge the deep grooves that dominate everyday actions. So, why are George Mason University and Central Missouri State University exceptional? Why do so many institutions want to be associated with renewal, yet so few seem able to renew?

I believe the answer is twofold, relating to both the individuals who populate the organization and the organization itself. On the individual level, there is the problem of "skilled incompetence," which has been so well articulated by Chris Argyris and Donald Schon.[6] As adults we get increasingly accomplished at protecting ourselves from the threat that reflection imposes. We tend to trap ourselves in defensive routines that insulate our basic assumptions from examination. The result is the wonderfully descriptive oxymoron—skilled incompetence. The better we become at defending the deep grooves that drive our thinking and behaviors, the worse we become at gaining new insights and learning. (See also lesson 12, "Know less, understand more.")

Ironically, according to Argyris and Schon, smart people are uniquely vulnerable to these defensive loops. Many professionals are almost always successful at what they do and rarely experience failure. Because of this, they have never learned how to learn from failure. When things go wrong, they become defensive, screen out criticism, and shift the blame to others. This defensive reasoning encourages individuals to keep private the premises and inferences that shape their behaviors, often hiding them even from themselves.

On the organizational level, there is a different kind of problem. Entropy is an inverse measure of a system's capacity for change. Isolated or closed systems move toward an end state of equilibrium, the point at which the system has exhausted all of its capacity for change. Open systems, in contrast, use disequilibrium to avoid deterioration. Disequilibrium typically comes in the form of external influences— ideas or people that offer new insights that challenge the status quo. Higher education has a tremendous problem here.

We have a distinct disregard for any ideas that are not sown and harvested in the fields of the academy. We use peer groups of similar schools for everything—in accreditation, in data sharing, in consortia. Either it never occurs to us or we just dismiss the notion of looking to United Airlines for ideas about registering people, to the Hilton Hotels for better ways to run our dormitories, or to Motorola University for innovative methods to enhance active learning. Instead, liberal arts college administrators go to conferences geared towards liberal arts college administrators. Community college people have their own

meetings. Research universities go another way, and religiously affili-
ated institutions still another. There is little chance for disequilibrium
because like-minded institutions and like-minded individuals are always speaking with each other.

Another aspect of this problem lies in how, as institutions, we train
and choose our leaders. College and university hiring practices are
designed to yield the ideal candidate, but who is the ideal candidate?
We see the ideal candidate as that individual who is best able to per-
sonify the traditions of the institution. A "representative" committee is
dutifully formed, applicants and nominations are solicited, and an ago-
nizing selection process is initiated. For a liberal arts college, the ideal
candidate received an undergraduate degree from a liberal arts college and went on to take a masters and Ph.D. degree in the humani-
ties. He or she received tenure as a professor at a liberal arts college
and was appointed department chair, then dean. The next required
stop was a vice presidency for academic affairs at another liberal arts
college. After six to eight years time-in-grade, a presidency becomes a
possibility. A similar narrowly focused career path could be described
for choosing a community college or research university leader. No
others need apply.

Such a recruitment process is perfectly designed to produce a leader
who reflects the beliefs, values, and norms of the institution as it has
been, not a leader who projects a vision of what the institution needs to
become. Hiring practices illustrate well the second law of thermodynamics, concerning closed systems and entropy. Little disequilibrium
is possible in this time-honored scenario that resonates with the wishes
of a conservation-oriented committee. Indeed, self-renewal and transformation are more wishful thinking than realistic possibilities in systems that are so well designed to venerate equilibrium.

In effect, our colleges and universities are caught in a double whammy:
we have very smart people in a very closed system. We have individuals
who are highly skilled at defensive reasoning working in institutions
that celebrate stability. Deep grooves are not only possible under such
conditions, they are highly predictable.

It is easy to dismiss the report in our story. It is not so easy to dismiss the ingrained routines and thinking patterns behind the way we plan and deliver our curriculum or the way we measure student success. Those unquestioned assumptions, along with many others embedded in the culture of a college campus, stand squarely in the path of quality and productivity improvement. The lesson "To create the future, challenge the past" does not advocate change for its own sake. All of us realize how threatening change can be. What the lesson does advocate, however, is a renewal process in which dialogue is used to bring deeply held assumptions to the surface. Only when these assumptions are clear can institutional members decide what is broken and needs to be discarded, what is bent and needs to be improved, and what is bountiful and needs to be preserved.

QUESTIONS

Think of a process within which you work. Ask yourself, Why is it done this way?

List the assumptions surrounding the way the process is currently done.

Bring together the people in the process. Engage each other in assumption-revealing dialogue. Then ask, What no longer works? What works but could be improved?

"Exceptional solutions to universal problems create universal problems."

Chris Newbold opened his office door, an office that he had called home for seven years. There were a few pink phone messages on the floor and a note from another professor. He gathered them up and stepped over to his desk. With an audible sigh, he pulled the chair back and made a slow descent.

Lunch had been a waste of money. He had bought a salad. Actually, Evan Ensign, an economics professor and fellow racquetball junkie, had bought it for him—he was too nervous to do more than rearrange the romaine. He tried to feign interest in the conversation that Evan was having with Matt Ostrowski, another economics professor, but his mind kept wandering.

Stretching his legs out in front of him, Chris leaned back in his chair and waited for the telephone call that the dean had promised to make to him. He closed his eyes and immediately had a flashback to eight years ago.

The interviewing process had been fun. Chris had visited four schools, all with excellent reputations. The presentations had gone well, and the fact that he was on-track to defend his dissertation and complete his Ph.D. by mid-June was a definite plus. Two schools offered him a position.

Chris discussed the choices with his wife, Margit. They decided to visit both schools and check out the communities. Their trip to the university was one of those memories that time never fades. After years of scratching and groveling through graduate school, he was given star treatment. The dean met them at the airport. Chris had lunch with six professors at the Mainline House in town. In the afternoon he met with the chief academic officer—the white-haired, venerable Dr. Amos Glass. Margit was taken on a real estate tour by two of the faculty members' wives. That evening they went to a basketball game. On the flight back home they decided. They canceled their trip to the other school.

The first two years were filled with highs and lows. A student yelling, "Dr. Newbold," as Chris walked on the quad gave him chills. Margit got pregnant and surprised him by sending a Happy Father's Day card to his office. Getting that very first "We are pleased to inform you . . ." letter that followed his submission of an article to a journal was thrilling.

But then there were his classes. He had been a teaching assistant in a large class during his last year in grad school; mostly he had graded papers and given quizzes—that was it for teaching preparation. At the university he had been given two lower-division courses. He was nervous and unsure of himself, and the student evaluations told the embarrassing story. He was characterized as "disorganized" and "did not stimulate the students' interest in the material."

Decent teaching evaluations were important to tenure, at least according to the faculty handbook and the supplemental booklet on procedures for appointments, reappointments, and promotions in Arts and Sciences. At times, though, Chris found it hard to believe that teaching counted a lot in tenure decisions. Chris knew he was struggling, but Dick Buss, a colleague in his department who was rumored to be a brutal teacher, flew through the tenure process. Of course, Dick was a publishing monster—15 major articles and two books in five years.

The next year Chris tried a bunch of new techniques in his classes. Some worked, and some bombed. His evaluations improved, but only slightly. On the positive side, a new push on his research was yielding good results. He and his coauthor had delivered several papers and had a major hit in a leading journal. The topic area was intriguing, and he enjoyed working with an economist.

Chris also became involved in a dormitory roundtable series. Of course, he didn't have much time—Stevie was almost three-years-old and Margit had returned to work on a part-time basis—but he really enjoyed the once-a-week evening discussion groups held in the dormitories. That is, he enjoyed them until Ed Graf, a full professor in his department, read a story in the student newspaper about the series in which Chris's name was mentioned. Ed's exact hallway comment was, "So, Chris, that research must be going great guns if you have time to spend your evenings in the dorms." Chris quit the group the very next day.

Last year and this year were a blur. He wanted tenure desperately. Margit and he were settled in, he loved the school, and Stevie was just starting kindergarten. The thought of having to leave sickened him, so he pushed hard. He helped organize a conference that was funded through an NEH grant, and he managed to get a few more articles published. A book that he edited was accepted for publication. He thought it would help, but he wasn't sure.

The official process began in September. A departmental committee reviewed a box of materials during the fall semester: his vita, six independent outside evaluations of his research, course and teaching evaluations, letters from colleagues, and copies of his publications. Chris was confident. Many people, both in his department and in others, told him he was a cinch.

That's why the results of the vote had been such a shock. He had been recommended, but it had been close. In a post-review meeting the dean explained that some members *of the department had been disturbed by the number of coauthored papers, especially those that were published with people outside of the discipline. The rap on him, according to the dean, was that he was floundering, that his research program had no focus.*

No focus? Too many coauthored papers? Chris felt side-swiped. He had never heard any of this before the conversation with the dean.

The recommendation from the department and the dean had gone forward to the Appointments, Promotions, and Tenure (AP&T) Committee in January. The 13-member committee, representing tenured full professors from across the university, met throughout the months of January and February. Chris tried to concentrate on his classes and family matters, but it was hard. Several decisions had already been made. A physics professor and an English professor were awarded tenure. Last week a popular music professor had been denied tenure and the student newspaper raised a huge stink. The waiting was tough.

Yesterday the dean said he thought the decision on Chris would be made the following afternoon. And so he sat—sick to his stomach, a bundle of raw nerves. He couldn't turn his brain off. His mind kept churning over the questions "What am I going to tell Margit?" "Where will we go?" "What could I have done differently?"

❖❖❖

Unlike some of the other stories in this book, there is nothing terribly unusual about this story. It is a straightforward tale about one individual's quest for tenure, a rite of passage into the academy of scholars. Nonetheless, the travails of Chris Newbold deserve our attention because they illustrate perfectly the kind of thinking that is compromising the performance of our colleges and universities.

Let's begin with a lesson 1 type of question: What is the aim of a tenure system? Most people would say the system is intended to ensure the quality of the faculty and, in turn, the quality of the institution. Does a tenure system do this? Is there any evidence that the mysterious, elaborate, and highly reverential process that Chris Newbold went through materially alters the quality of the faculty in the aggregate? The answer is a clear-cut no. People who administer tenure systems, as well as most other processes and systems in our colleges and universities, do not understand that a central problem in management and leadership is the inability to understand variation or the deviation between planned goals and observed outcomes (this would occur in the check phase—check to see whether carrying out the plan yields the desired improvement—of a PDCA cycle described in an earlier lesson). We need to think very, very hard about the information that is contained in variation.

All failures to achieve a desired level of quality stem from two sources of variation: they are attributable either to the system or to causes external to the system. System failures are "common" causes of variation because every participant in the system is at risk of experiencing a systemic problem. Extrasystemic failures, in contrast, are assignable to fleeting events or "special" causes. A quick example: an automobile veers off the road and almost causes an accident. A special-cause explanation would be the driver's inexperience or a few too many cocktails; a common-cause explanation would be a faulty steering mechanism. The difference between the two sources of variation becomes clear when we think of how we might eliminate the problem. In the first case, we would have the driver attend driving school or alcoholic counseling. Would either of these approaches be appropriate if the problem was with the steering? Of course not. If the steering mechanism is faulty, the car will always end up in the ditch regardless of who is driving because the problem is embedded in the system.

In organizations, researchers estimate that special variation causes 15 percent of the problems in processes, while common variation causes the remaining 85 percent. W. Edwards Deming is even more extreme.

He estimates that 94 percent of problems and possibilities for improvement belong to the system. In his opinion, only a tiny fraction of the variance, 6 percent, can be assigned to extrasystemic failures.[1]

In spite of these numbers, most organizations operate as if the reverse were true. The operating assumption is that the best way to reduce variability and increase quality is to find someone to blame. This assumption is based on the theory of bad apples.[2] According to the theory, quality is best achieved by discovering bad apples and reprimanding them or removing them from the lot. Here is how the theory is applied. First, you devise a peer review system to develop rankings, a distribution that attempts to measure a group of people (or departments or institutions) based on one or more quality factors. The next step is to establish a threshold to separate acceptable quality (which does not require action) from unacceptable quality (which requires action). This quality-by-threshold approach is, in effect, an inspection system enforced by a search for deficiencies. Devotees of this approach honestly believe that by developing a distribution (a ranking activity that measures variance) and then eliminating the tail end, the overall quality of the distribution will improve significantly.

This "sort and shoot" inspection methodology is intuitively appealing. After all, there is great rhetoric involved. You have standards. You are willing to make tough decisions in order to eliminate offending behaviors. But, if Deming is correct and most problems are attributable to the system, eliminating statistical outliers has little influence on the aggregate because the variability in the system is not greatly affected by extrasystemic problems. Make the calculation yourself. Put 6 percent in the tail end of a normal distribution. Draw a line that represents a mean and another that shows the 6 percent threshold. Now, eliminate the statistical outliers—those individuals who demonstrate unacceptable levels of quality—and recalculate the mean. How much does it change? Only 6 percent.

Do we, in higher education, practice sort and shoot? All the time. Accrediting agencies have used traditional notions of peer review to generate rankings based on a series of quality indicators such as the number of books in the library collection or the number of Ph.D.s on the faculty. Federal and state agencies and governing boards often use comparability data to exercise control. For example, the new Campus Security Act, which is intended to reduce the incidence of crime on campus, requires colleges to report various crime statistics. The idea is that tail-end institutions with poor crime records will be encouraged by exposure to public scrutiny to improve their safety records. Professors who grade "on a curve" and who engage in passionate debates over the evils of grade inflation are practicing another brand of quality-by-threshold. And then there is the tenure system.

Think back to Professor Newbold. He was part of a system at his institution for seven years. That system, like all systems, has variation in it. Specifically, there is a distribution of talent on campus that includes great professors, not-so-great professors, and bottom-of-the-barrel professors. The tenure process might conclude that Professor Newbold's talent was below the threshold (unacceptable quality); then action would need to be taken. Presumably, if Professor Newbold had written a number of additional articles (or had avoided the deadly sin of coauthorship) or received slightly higher teaching evaluations, his performance would have bumped him up to an acceptable level and no action would have been required.

Again, will the tenure system's ability to identify Professor Newbold as a bad apple and eliminate him from the lot change the quality of the professoriate in the aggregate? Will it help us achieve our aim of improving the quality of the faculty and the institution? No, it will not. A bad apple approach, based on a doctrine of improvement by elimination, has a limited ability to enhance the quality of the faculty or the institution because the overall level of quality is determined by the system, not by its outliers.

A more productive way to approach the issue would be to ask, What are the possible "common" causes of failure in the tenure case? There are many. Consider the hiring process. Is the hiring process—including the generation of a pool of candidates, the use of various criteria to screen candidates, and the department's voting procedures—designed to ensure that the candidate with the best possible chance of gaining tenure is offered the position? How about teaching? If we evaluate someone on his or her teaching, does the faculty development system have specific mechanisms in place to facilitate the transition from a bottom-of-the-barrel teacher to a great teacher? Does the system help identify "best practices" in teaching and encourage the individual to improve? If scholarship is a criterion, how does the system communicate scholarship aims and support a professor's acquisition of the needed research skills to meet those aims? The list of potential problems common to everyone on a tenure track is extensive.

Although the rules of the tenure game were never defined, Professor Newbold and other tenure track professors were forced to play and win or else be eliminated. They were exposed to a system of traditional peer review that treats all problems as extrasystemic problems—isolated, idiosyncratic, and assignable to an individual.

To me, the most troubling aspect of this inspection methodology is the inability of bad apple theorists to understand that because they are focusing on adequacy, excellence necessarily eludes them. Again, think about the distribution of talent on Professor Newbold's campus. If it is *possible* to function at a "great professor" level, why is it *acceptable* to function at a "not-so-great" level? Every time a professor fails to perform at the higher level of quality, the institution wastes resources. Students don't learn at the rate they could and research output is less than optimal. The most egregious waste of all is the time, energy, and money devoted to building the elaborate bureaucracies necessary to give "sort and shoot" approaches their trappings of legitimacy and effectiveness. Tenure, for example, is a maze of rules and rituals: policy manuals are produced, committees are organized, and appeal procedures are outlined. The copier runs hot from all the articles and vitae that are duplicated and distributed. All of these activities are necessary to support threshold decisions that have minimal effect on the quality of the institution.

Our continued reliance on quality-by-threshold means that as institutions we are asking the wrong question. We ask whether we are good enough instead of whether we are the best we can be. In our story, the institution is asking whether Professor Newbold is good enough to be admitted into the academy instead of whether the professoriate is the best it can be.

Wouldn't it be better to redirect the resources used to perform an after-the-fact inspection to before-the-fact improvement, to focus on the whole group instead of the tail end, and to encourage and include rather than punish and eliminate? Our time and energy should be devoted to devising a methodology—a learning cycle, if you will—that can improve the quality of the entire crop of apples by 20 percent, or even 30 to 40 percent, not a methodology that is fixated on exposing the few bad apples.

Instead of quality-by-threshold, we need quality-by-improvement. We need to adopt a theory of management and process improvement that views the distribution of quality, from better to worse, as a chance to learn about the whole system. This systemic view would enable us to reduce variation and shift the distribution so that real gains are possible. Our bad apple story provides a perfect illustration. How would we proceed if we wanted to improve the quality of the teaching and learning process by 40 percent? As we have seen, an inspection approach concentrates all its energies on the tail end of the distribution. Quality-by-threshold sees poor performers as bad apples in what otherwise is a good system. Quality-by-improvement, however, assumes that everyone wants to do, and is capable of doing, a good job[2]; poor performers are seen as good apples caught in a not-so-good system.

Let's look at three learning strategies that can bring about systemic improvement. First, organizations can develop the kind of tight feedback loops described in lesson 7. Without feedback, we cannot take corrective action. We cannot adapt and grow. What is the nature of feedback on teaching in higher education? Most institutions rely solely on student ratings. Unfortunately, most such rating systems are devised by administrators, conducted at the end of the semester, analyzed so that professors can be ranked, and returned weeks or even months later. Such feedback methods have everything to do with thresholds and accountability and nothing to do with improvement. A better approach is the one being taken at the U.S. Air Force Academy. The faculty members there have developed a student critique to provide instructors with systematic feedback about the effect they have had on students' knowledge, thinking, and attitudes. The comprehensive 43-item instrument is administered at the end of the semester and returned directly to professors within two days. Administrators have no access to the results. What has been the effect of the new student evaluations? Perceived effectiveness of instruction throughout the institution has increased by more than 20 percent in two years.

A second learning strategy is to increase our understanding of the extended process. Taking snapshots, like student critiques, and sharing those snapshots with professors can be an effective method for improving the teaching performance of the professoriate as a whole. The only problem is that a snapshot does not capture the series of events leading up to the picture as a video camera is capable of doing. The video camera equivalent to systemic improvement on a college campus is to study the process as a whole. At Delaware County Community College (DCCC), faculty and administrators have begun to study the full-time faculty hiring process. Why? Because if, for example, an institution valued great teaching skills above all else, should it not have a hiring process that does an exceptional job of identifying those applicants with the greatest teaching potential? DCCC has reached that conclusion. The college is studying its process—mapping it, identifying various performance indicators, tracking individuals, and seeking ways to improve the process.

A final learning strategy entails a fervent search for best practices.[3] Rather than looking for and attacking bad efforts, a systematic quality-by-improvement approach seeks to identify and study best efforts. By linking high-quality outcomes with the processes that produced them, good apple theorists are able to understand the dynamics of what constitutes best practices and learn from them. The next step is to institutionalize best practices by communicating what has been learned to the entire distribution. Colleges and universities must be humble enough to admit that other organizations are better at some things and wise enough to try to learn from and even surpass them. This approach could be limited to an internal study of, say, best teaching practices. It could entail an analysis of a few direct competitors or peers or a broad comparison to general trends across a much larger group of related institutions.

In the case of Samford University, an institution devoted to undergraduate teaching excellence, the strategy includes best-in-class benchmarking based on studies of organizations with reputations for delivering exceptional services to their customers. Last year, Samford faculty and administrators decided that they wanted to use the Malcolm Baldrige National Quality Award criteria as an assessment tool for their upcoming Southern Association of Colleges and Schools accreditation self-study. In a typically humble and wise fashion, the senior leadership of Samford drove from Birmingham, Alabama, to Kingsport, Tennessee (the home of Eastman Chemical, a 1993 Baldrige Award–winning company) for a two-day "learning opportunity." The aim, again was to provide exceptional services to students; the strategy was a search for best practices.

The tight feedback loops at the U.S. Air Force Academy, the increased understanding of extended processes at DCCC, and Samford's search for best practices are useful ways of helping to make the shift from an environment that stresses thresholds and enforcement to an environment that emphasizes reflection and improvement. The shift is from punishing and eliminating to encouraging and including, from a specific focus on the tail end of the distribution to a general appreciation for the distribution as a whole.

The outcome of the telephone call to Professor Newbold will have tremendous consequences for him and for his family, but, contrary to accepted campus thinking and in spite of all the resources thrown at the decision process, the tenure decision will have little bearing on the quality of the institution. That is because the administration is attempting to improve the institution by pursuing an exceptional solution to what is a universal problem. And it will not work.

QUESTIONS

Identify all the areas in your institution where you rely on standards, thresholds, and peer review to judge quality.

Identify individuals or programs that have failed to meet those standards and then ask, How did the system fail them?

Do you have a methodology to identify best practices in teaching, curriculum design, advising, and so on?

Do you regularly ask, Is this a people problem or a process problem?

"Universal solutions to exceptional problems create universal problems."

These were unusually hot days for August in Pennsylvania. Earlier in the week the thermometer had reached a slow boil. By two in the afternoon yesterday the mercury had punched its way to 92° as Tracie Reeb, a 19-year-old sopho-more, weeded flower beds at the college in her jeans and long-sleeved shirt.

She wasn't complaining. She was grateful to have the work-study job. The extra cash would come in handy next year. But, she thought, there would be no next year if she died of heat prostration while fussing over marigolds. After a few last gulps of morning coffee, she slipped into a pair of shorts and pulled a tank top over her head. Maybe a little more breathing room would help as she prepared herself for another day on dandelion patrol.

❖

Jannette Nelson's desk was positioned right next to President Mark Bruce's door. It was a small college, so everyone pretty much knew everyone else. That was both a blessing and a curse. The blessing: she could usually get a problem solved with one phone call. The curse: most other people on campus thought that the best way to get a problem solved was to march in and see the president, hence the strategic location of her desk.

Today Jannette had outflanked an angry Morris Platt. He was a trustee of the college who had a complaint (actually he had a lot of complaints, but since he had promised the college $3 million, everyone's hearing had miraculously improved). Fortunately, the president had taken his wife and kids on a beat-the-heat drive to the shore, which left Jannette to deal with Mr. Platt's urgent problem.

❖

Doug Bacon, the recently hired vice president for business affairs, had just gotten off the phone with the president's office. The contractor had confirmed that the new dorm would not be ready for fall classes, the utility bill for August looked like it might equal the size of the endowment, a "risk management" meeting that should have had an aspirin break on the agenda had taken a two-hour chunk out of his afternoon, and now this. The last thing he needed was a messy little political problem.

Doug had already had a run-in with Platt at the last board meeting. Platt had repeatedly interrupted his budget presentation with statements like, "We don't do things like that at my company."

❖

"So, let me get this straight," said Ernie Becerril, the college's physical plant director, "Some member of the board saw what?"

Doug Bacon repeated, "He saw some girl, young, looked like a student, working in those flowers by the main gate. He says the girl might as well have been naked. She had on a tank top—not a regular T-shirt—and overly short shorts." Ernie listened in amazement. "So he goes directly to the president's office," Bacon continued. "Jannette said he lectured her for 15 minutes about moral values and the kind of message we were sending."

Ernie paused a moment and then said, "Well, I think I know the girl you're talking about. Her name's Tracie. But, Doug, it's a zillion degrees out there. The shorts weren't that short."

"I understand, Ernie, but you don't see the guys over there running around with their butts hanging out."

"Well, the older guys always wear khakis during the summer, but some of the younger guys—Danny, Ray, Terry—wear shorts when it's hot. You know, they wear what's comfortable."

Doug listened and winced. His head was about to split open like a ripe watermelon on a sidewalk. "Look, I understand that. But you need to do something," he snapped. "I don't want Platt having any more seizures over semi-naked students. Okay?"

"Okay," said Ernie.

❖

The workers from physical plant huddled over their beers. They alternated between taking sips and taking shots at the administration, especially Bacon, the new guy. They hadn't had a raise because of budget problems in two years. Now this.

The policy had been circulated earlier in the day. As of next week, they would be required to wear long-sleeved shirts and full-length pants year-round. There had been no explanations; marching orders had just been given. On one of the hottest days of the year, they had been told to button up. Was this some sort of joke? No, actually, it wasn't. They had been assured the policy was for real and that anyone who violated it could expect that action would be taken.

Another pitcher of beer arrived at the table.

After several minutes of renewed sipping and snipping, Terry announced to the table that he felt chills. "Yep," he said. "I'm definitely coming down with something. Summer cold. Just came on me. Yesterday I felt fine and now I don't."

Ray, one of Terry's best friends, chimed in, "You know, I don't feel so good myself. Something must be going around."

❖

On the following Monday, the president ended his cabinet meeting a little early. These days, with this heat and humidity, no one seemed to have much energy. As he walked by Jannette's desk she said, "Have you heard? The entire physical plant called in sick today. Something about a new dress code policy."

❖❖❖

Just as Doug Bacon was saying, "I don't want Platt having any more seizures over semi-naked students," I hope that bells and whistles began going off in the reader's head. After our extensive discussion of the causes of variation in the previous lesson, readers should have been pulling their hair out by the end of the story, screaming at both Doug and Ernie, "You blew it! The incident was special; it was extrasystemic, just a simple, random occurrence."

To review, W. Edwards Deming says there are two sources of loss that result from the confusion of special causes of variation with common causes. They are

1. Ascribing a variation or mistake to a special cause when in fact the cause belongs to the system (common cause)
2. Ascribing a variation or mistake to the system (common cause) when in fact the cause was special[1]

All through the previous lesson there was evidence that pointed to the system (common cause): Chris Newbold was offered positions at two excellent institutions, he worked hard at the university, he never was certain what the expectations were, and there were surprises along the way. There was no evidence of faculty development or organizational learning. There was, however, overwhelming evidence to suggest that if Chris were eventually found lacking, the fault would have been attributed to him. The question around his department and on campus would have been "Why did Professor Newbold fail?" not "How did the system fail him?"

The story in this lesson describes a dramatically different situation in the study of variation. It was unusually hot. Tracie was a part-timer, a work-study student. Platt was a chronic complainer. The basic standard of dress was stable and appropriate. All the bits and pieces of data pointed to a special circumstance, but the new policy "ascribed a variation or a mistake to the system (common cause) when in fact the cause was special." The result was predictable—frustration, hurt, and anger— all because management failed to distinguish between a random and nonrandom event. In essence, despite all the administrative brainpower available, no one simply went to our comfortably clothed sophomore and said, "Tracie, I need you to wear something a bit less revealing tomorrow."

Higher education, it would seem, has a penchant for this type of misclassification—attempting to respond to an isolated incident by altering a system or process. One reason is our organizational structure and culture. In a loosely coupled system, administrators who are responsible for small chunks of territory have limited access to system information. Their perspective is truncated by barriers. Still, operating in the narrow confines of their isolated boxes, they are expected to be consummate problem solvers. They are rewarded for being decisive, for detecting and correcting errors. It should not be surprising, therefore, that when faced with a problem most administrators are unable and unwilling to pursue the common versus special cause line of inquiry. They are unable because they cannot easily generate information to establish the degree of randomness; they are unwilling because the reward system values a quick response over a thorough response.

In addition to structure and culture difficulties, an externally driven phenomenon has taken center stage in recent years. As colleges and universities have come under increasing public scrutiny for their procedures, from golden parachutes for senior administrators to questionable course offerings and speech codes, administrators have become correspondingly skittish and reactionary. An unpleasant incident with a fraternity or a clerk who manages to abscond with funds from the business office will prompt wholesale changes and fervent testimonials from those in charge, "That will never, ever happen here again." In such a highly sensitized environment, accidents (or random events) are not allowed. Each and every mistake results in a heavy blanket of new policies.

An obvious question at this point might be, How can we distinguish between the two different causes of variation? One of the best ways to tease out this information is to use a control chart.[2] All processes operate within a range. No human being can repeat the same task in the same way taking the same amount of time. It is impossible, even for a robot. Thus, every process has a normal range within which it operates. A control chart provides a graphic illustration of variation in a process, both random variation and nonrandom variation. We can create a control chart by graphing the fluctuating points and then drawing statistically determined upper and lower control limits on either side of the process average. Those fluctuations that occur within the control limits are random events resulting from common causes within the system. They can only be affected by changing the system. Points or spikes outside the limits, however, come from special causes and are not part of the normal way the process operates. In effect, a control chart sends out statistical signals which we can use to detect the existence of a special cause or to determine whether the observed changes are chance variation attributable to the system.

Take quiz grades, for example. You can total the grades for your students and derive an average each time you give a quiz. Would you expect the average to remain the same from quiz to quiz? Of course not. Randomness (75, 78, 82, 76) is expected because it is built into the system. The material changes, the questions vary, and the students' work load shifts. It is not possible to remove random variation. It is possible, however, to improve significantly the distribution (92, 88, 89,

90) by changing the system, perhaps by having a mandatory review session before each quiz.

But what happens when a 24-hour flu or a Final Four appearance by the university's basketball team occurs the night before the quiz? Our normal fluctuation of quiz averages might now include a 33, which has a special cause, nonrandom in nature and immune from any well-intentioned system change.

In their book *Total Quality Improvement Guide for Institutions of Higher Education*, Robert Cornesky and Samuel McCool use an illustration from the building and grounds division at a state university to demonstrate the use of control charts in identifying common and special causes of variation.[3] In their example, the director of the division wanted to know why work orders were not being completed on time. So, each day the number of incomplete work orders was recorded. After a month, the director began calculating the average and then deriving the upper and lower control limits. The chart indicated a normal fluctuation around the mean with two spikes—on day 1 and day 14. What was unique or special about these days? According to Cornesky and McCool, after the director examined what had occurred on those two days, he discovered that on both days a new employee had started work—a carpenter on day 1 and an electrician on day 14. After further reflection and analysis, the director concluded that neither employee had been given the proper training in how to prioritize work or fill out the work order forms. The solution was simple. The director introduced a training session for new employees so that they could learn the right way to do things from the very beginning.

The building and grounds scenario suggests not only that common causes and special causes require different treatment, but also that the methods for determining the appropriate treatment are different. A problem that results from a special cause is localized and unusual. The problem-solving approach entails the following:

1. Work with timely data so that special causes are identified early.
2. Upon finding a problem resulting from a special cause, search immediately for unusual occurences.

3. Seek to eliminate the temporary or local problem; do not make fundamental changes in the process or system.

4. Take steps to prevent the special cause from recurring.[4]

Much of what we do in higher education does not lend itself to the exactness of data gathering and control chart analysis. Nonetheless, by understanding the information in variation and asking the right questions, colleges and universities can avoid many of the problems that result from applying common-cause solutions to special-cause problems (and vice versa). The methodology is not exact, but inquiry into the nature of problems—before rushing off to a solution—usually leads to important insights.

A useful illustration comes from the University of Wisconsin—Madison's graduate school. Each month at its regular meetings the board of regents asked the graduate school for a report on research funding. The numbers fluctuated wildly from month to month—up $5 million, down $10 million, up $40 million, and down $30 million. Each month the regents asked why there were fluctuations, and the dean of the graduate school tried to offer a plausible explanation.

One month, the dean gathered monthly data for the last 10 years. He plotted the level of grant funds awarded each month on a simple run chart (data points plotted over time). The chart suggested that grant monies increased, on average, 1 percent per month, but each year two months were unusual: September and December. September peaked millions above every other month, and December hit an annual low. Why? After scrutinizing years worth of Septembers, the dean decided that the large jump in funding was assignable to WARF (Wisconsin Alumni Research Funds) which were allocated every September. In December, granting agencies slowed down for the holidays.

In this instance, while the two months did show spikes of activity, it was all part of a cyclical pattern. The monthly variation was part of the system, so it made no sense to react to September peaks and December valleys. The activity was stable and predictable. Knowing this, the board and the dean could shift their attention from trying to reduce the month-to-month variation to improving the average, which meant improving the system by which the institution identified, applied for, and fulfilled research grant contracts.

This same issue of trying to distinguish between common causes and special causes of variation was a recent subject of concern at Rio Salado Community College. Rio Salado has a strategic planning steering team that selects processes for improvement from prioritized lists submitted by various project identification committees. The committees, in turn, receive recommendations for process improvements from a number of sources, including individual employees, improvement teams, accreditation self-study reports, and analyses of regular surveys of faculty, students, and staff. One project was selected on the basis of a few annoying experiences with the college's voice mail system. The team assigned to improve the process conducted a special survey of all employees to determine the extent of the problem. According to Pam Walter, the institutional research coordinator at the college, "After reviewing the results, the team determined that the problem was not with the system but with how a few people in the organization were using it." She added, "In other words, we were dealing with a people problem, not a process problem."[5] In contrast to the University of Wisconsin—Madison case, this situation did involve a special cause, and the solution involved isolating the special cause for a one-time fix, working directly with the few people who were misusing the system.

Finally, I would like to return to W. Edwards Deming for a moment. When speaking about variation, he states there are losses that stem from the confusion of special causes and common causes. What exactly are these losses? In the previous lesson, where a common cause was treated as a special cause, the losses were related to demoralization. Most people know the feeling that comes from being blamed for something that is largely out of their control. They find it frustrating and demeaning. Professor Newbold, if he doesn't get tenure, will know this feeling all too well. Even if he does get tenure, he is likely to be embittered by what has happened to him. The tenure experience will have a direct impact on his performance. Being trapped in an inequitable system saps people's energy and has a direct and measurable impact on the quality and quantity of their work. There are also direct losses: the monetary costs associated with developing and administering a tenure system are not insignificant, and the costs of increased complexity are evident in the time and energy associated with identifying bad apples like Professor Newbold, instead of nurturing a comprehensive faculty development effort.

What are the losses from this lesson? Let me quote Deming here, "If anyone adjusts a stable process to try to compensate for a result that is undesirable, or for a result that is extra good, the output that follows will be worse than if he had left the process alone."[6] At the urging of the vice president, the physical plant director in our story tampered with a stable process and the losses began accumulating almost immediately. Productivity went to zero because everyone in the physical plant mysteriously came down with a summer cold. Even when the physical plant workers come back, after the administration rescinds its idiotic policy, their work ethic will remain low. They feel betrayed and unappreciated, hassled and belittled, and they will not forget. The drop in productivity is the heavy penalty that the administration will pay for applying a universal solution to what was an exceptional problem.

QUESTIONS

What are some examples of special- and common-cause variation at your institution?

What would be the best way to distinguish between special and common causes of variation before a decision is made?

How can you ensure that everyone is aware of the difference between random and nonrandom events and acts accordingly?

LESSON 12

"Know less, understand more."

Tony had never been a great student, but he did try. He usually got C's, sometimes a B, and occasionally a D. Still, as he looked down at the grades he'd just received for the last semester, he was shocked—one C and two F's. "What do I do now?" he asked himself.

He had loans and grants. They wouldn't pay for F's, and he had no money himself. He would have to take some time off, drop out, and hope that he could come back in a few semesters. He looked again at the grade card. Two F's? Why?

He knew why. He didn't have time to study; he was working four nights a week at a local motel and waiting tables on the weekends. Every extra moment he spent studying. He was bleary-eyed most of the time. Exhausted. Why?

Because his school work load this semester was much tougher than before. One class was pretty much what he had expected, but the other two had overwhelmed him. They were both courses in his major. Unfortunately, he wasn't prepared for either of them. From the very beginning, the professors in these courses were discussing things that

had not been covered in the prerequisite courses the semester before. Tony found himself doing extra reading, asking
other students for help, or trying to figure stuff out on his
own. He just wasn't prepared.

Why?

Because the professors of those prerequisite courses were
recently hired part-timers. They had been given a time slot, a
classroom, a textbook, and a hearty "welcome aboard." That
was it. They worked hard to develop a syllabus that covered
the textbook and allowed them to discuss issues that they
thought were important, based on their own work experiences. None of their quick-study preparation involved
meeting with other professors, so the part-timers didn't
know what the teachers of the next-in-line courses expected
their students to know.

Why?

Because the department didn't have an orientation session
for new hires. The part-timers were never acquainted with
the curriculum or program objectives or the mission of the
department. They didn't know where they fit in. Because the
part-timers taught mostly night classes and the professors
mostly day, it wasn't even likely that the two groups would
bump into each other in the hallway. Also, policy did not
allow part-timers to attend department meetings; they were
just for the professors.

Why?[1]

❖❖❖

In any given year, at any given college or university, there are hundreds of Tonys. They drop out for a few semesters, come back, drop
out again. Some ultimately graduate; others get sidetracked and never
complete their course work. Many of them earn their D's and F's. They
try to slide by, cram in a few hours of reading before an exam or skip
out on team assignments. You know the type. But that wasn't Tony; he
tried his best.

If the aim of higher education, as we discussed in the very first lesson, is success for each student, the most important question we can ask as an institution is, Why did Tony fail? But we don't. There is a complete disconnection between Tony's failure and the way the institution goes about its work. If we were a manufacturer and many of our components were rejected in the quality assurance process, wouldn't we be stumbling all over ourselves trying to figure out why? We certainly wouldn't just say, "Well, must be a bad part," and continue to operate the production line as is. If we were a financial institution and we lost a series of large deposits, wouldn't we start asking questions? Or would we just ignore the situation and continue on—business as usual?

Why do we tolerate such poor performance in higher education and never look for a cause? Why do we speak about excellence in education and never address our shortfalls? Why can't we learn to do better?

Learning encompasses two dimensions. The first dimension, operational learning, is the acquisition of a skill, which implies a physical ability to produce some action. The second dimension, conceptual learning, is the ability to articulate a conceptual understanding of an experience. Both dimensions are important: what people know (competence) and what they understand (meaning). Daniel Kim, an expert on learning in the context of an organization, has used the example of a carpenter to illustrate the distinction between operational and conceptual learning.[2] A carpenter who has mastered the skills of woodworking without understanding the concept of building coherent structures like tables and houses cannot use those skills effectively. Similarly, a carpenter who possesses vast knowledge about architecture and design but who has few complementary skills to carry out designs cannot effectively use that knowledge. Making the connection, then, between thought (know-why) and action (know-how) is the key to most learning opportunities.

The ability to cycle back and forth between competence and meaning is particularly important in a dynamic environment. The developing person, a carpenter or anyone else, must not only continually acquire new levels of competence to deal effectively with a changing environment but also learn the reasons behind events. Such a coupling enables the individual to respond to new situations and conditions.

Learning ultimately involves increasing our capacity to change based on a set of possible outcomes (effective and ineffective). When we compare these possible outcomes with the learning dimensions (competence and meaning), the lesson embedded in the story—"Know less, understand more"—begins to take shape in a series of scenarios that represent the interaction of each of the two learning dimensions and the two outcomes.

The first scenario, demonstrating success, results from linking competence with an effective outcome. It is illustrated as follows:

Learning		**Outcome**		
Competence	+	Effective	=	Demonstrating Success

The world of higher education is one in which we are continually being asked to demonstrate success. The teacher-student relationship is illustrative. Professors lecture on a topic. Students are then asked to show—in the form of an examination, paper, or laboratory test—that they have mastered the material. If students can show a minimal level of competence, they are awarded a passing grade. In this case, operational learning has lead to an effective outcome; students have demonstrated success by showing that they have acquired skills.

Demonstrating success is the dominant learning-outcome paradigm in higher education. Being able to pass a course is largely an exercise in proving competence; being able to gain tenure is also an exercise in proving competence. We are stuck on know-how and we worship at the altar of effectiveness. Demonstrating success is a deep groove in our culture, one that begins with the SAT and other entrance exams and continues through senior theses and Ph.D. dissertations. But what about the other interactions? For example, what is the nature of the association between meaning and an effective outcome?

This combination involves the notion of explaining success. Instead of acquiring a skill, as was the case in the first scenario, this combination couples a conceptual understanding of events—or know-why learning—with an effective outcome. The relationship looks like this:

Learning   **Outcome**

Meaning   +   Effective   =   Explaining Success

For the most part, explaining success is seen to be an irrelevant exercise in higher education. The student who does well, does well. The professor who gets tenure, gets tenure. There are few attempts to understand why, to discover the reasons behind the effective outcome. This is unfortunate. Being able to explain the factors that undergird the success of some can obviously enhance the chances of others if those practices are shared. Learning why one student does well or why a particular professor received tenure can uncover a series of best practices that can be used to improve the performance of those who are struggling to succeed.

Next, there is the relationship between competence and an ineffective outcome: demonstrating failure. It is illustrated in the following manner:

Learning   **Outcome**

Competence   +   Ineffective   =   Demonstrating Failure

Whereas explaining success is usually perceived as irrelevant in higher education, demonstrating failure is simply unwise. We flunk our failures. This stands in sharp contrast with both science and industry. For example, trial and error has been a research methodology in many scientific advancements. In industry, marketing researchers have successfully used prototypes of products to elicit negative reactions. In both instances, failure is seen as a practical outcome of experimentation. It is an interim step that extends knowledge by demonstrating, for all to see, what does not work. Needless to say, such an approach to knowledge development and operational learning does not receive much positive attention on a college campus.

Finally, there is explaining failure, the interaction of conceptual learning and an ineffective outcome. It looks like this:

Learning		**Outcome**	
Meaning	+	Ineffective =	Explaining Failure

The potential for growth and transformation that resides in explaining failure is tremendous, because an ineffective outcome enables people within the system to reflect their shared assumptions. The process is a learning cycle consisting of generating a concrete experience (in this case, an ineffective outcome), making observations about and reflecting on that experience (asking why), forming abstract concepts and generalizations based on those reflections, and testing those ideas in a new situation.

While demonstrating success is the dominant learning paradigm in higher education, explaining failure may be the most effective learning paradigm. We need look no further than Tony for evidence to support this contention. What did the institution learn from Tony's inability to demonstrate success? Nothing. As it stands, he is just a statistic, a kid who couldn't make it. Further, his failure confirms some people's belief that the institution has tough standards, that it has not succumbed to the dreaded disease of grade inflation. But if we put know-how on the back burner for a second and think about know-why, we might ask, What could the organization learn from Tony's failure? This question puts a different spin on an ineffective outcome. Tony's two F's provide a learning opportunity for the organization. First, the school might reflect on why he didn't succeed. Maybe it's not simply his fault; maybe there is a common cause (recall Chris Newbold, the professor in lesson 10—"Exceptional solutions to universal problems create universal problems"). By studying the situation and gathering information on root causes, the organization might form a series of hypotheses based on this reflection. For example, does the way the institution hires, orients, and integrates part-time professors into the delivery of the curriculum affect student success?

Another way to think of explaining failure is in terms of Chris Argyris's notion of single-loop versus double-loop learning. [3] Whenever an error is detected and corrected without questioning or altering the underlying values of the system, the learning is single loop. Argyris uses a thermostat to explain. A thermostat is programmed to detect states of "too cold" or "too hot," and to correct the situation by turning the heat on or off. Tony's situation might stimulate this level of learning. An analysis of grades could determine that several professors are flunking too many students, or a budget review might indicate that the institution is not retaining students. Corrections could then be made. The professors might lower their standards for passing or schedule more review sessions the next semester. A task force might be formed to address new ways to bolster retention.

Double-loop learning is more in-depth and involves questioning the system itself and the reasons for the failures. A thermostat that could ask, "Why am I set at 68 degrees?" and then explore whether some other temperature might more economically achieve the aim of making the room more comfortable would be engaged in double-loop learning. For Tony—and all other students—a double-loop learning environment that emphasizes explaining failures, not merely demonstrating successes, is the best chance for continuously improving the quality of their educational experience.

So, why don't we ask, "Why is the thermostat set at 68 degrees?" or "Why did Tony fail?" Why don't we spend as much time, or more, explaining failure as we do demonstrating success? I am sure there are a number of complex explanations, but, for the sake of simplicity and space, let's consider two. First, it is simply a whole lot easier to blame Tony. Higher education is neither better nor worse at playing the "blame game" than other organizations. Problem solving by its very nature is messy business. Few people really enjoy tackling difficult issues. We know this from decision theory. People have the marvelous ability to identify problems that require their attention. They also make a subconscious practice of generating a mental listing from most critical to least critical. Next, they roll up their sleeves and, with grit and gusto, proceed to attack the bottom of the list—the least critical. Why? Because it makes them feel good. They can solve problems—whole bunches of little problems—while avoiding those messy brain-busters at the top of the list.

Given this predisposition, it should not be surprising that the questioning stops after the most convenient answer is provided. Why did Tony fail? Tony is the culprit; he was not prepared. No need to look further. Next problem.

So, the first reason we tolerate Tony's failure is because it is important for us—administrators, professors—to dismiss any personal culpability in the matter. Once we have exonerated ourselves, there is obviously no reason to engage in any difficult double-loop self-reflection.

The second reason we tolerate Tony's failure is because he represents a proximate answer to the question *why*. Often, especially in complex systems, there is a large gap between cause and effect. Take our recent infatuation with what has come to be known as "three strikes and you're out" legislation. Citizens perceive that crime is out of control, and politicians want to get reelected. The result is well-intended legislation designed to "get tough on crime" by locking up three-time felons for 25 years to life. Unfortunately, the seeds of today's antisocial behavior were sown a decade or more ago—inadequate education, a lack of economic opportunity, unwanted pregnancies. "Three strikes" is a political palliative that will end up costing billions but will do nothing to solve the underlying cause of crime.

Tony's situation has a similar temporal quality. His decision to drop out occurred several weeks after the end of a semester, while the prerequisite courses that failed to prepare him were taken the previous semester. Further, the development of a precise set of learning outcomes for the prerequisite courses and a new-instructor orientation session should have happened well before the previous semester. The effect of these past failures, however, is occurring now, so the tendency is to look for a proximate explanation, one that is close at hand—Tony simply wasn't prepared.

There are many other explanations, ranging from some of the negative side effects of academic freedom to issues relating to process own-

ership (discussed in lesson 3). Nonetheless, important questions remain: How do we create an environment in which explaining failure is
a well-accepted theme? How can we make the issue of Tony's failure
resonate through our colleges and universities?

One approach I am particularly fond of is the rhetoric and methodology of a "diagnostic journey." Quite a few individuals in the health
care field suggest that quality improvement consists of defining a problem, making a diagnosis, administering a remedy, and then holding
the gains.[4] Such a diagnostic journey can be short and sweet or long
and tortuous. The critical point, however, is that the word *diagnostic*
means understanding the fundamental nature of a problem, and *journey* implies a series of steps.

A wonderful, and ironic, example of a diagnostic journey involves
the efforts of the University of Pennsylvania and its concern with the
cost of trash removal on campus:

First, there is the problem definition stage:

- Initial statement of the problem: The costs of trash removal are
  too high. The city is considering the elimination of a special
  exemption for nonprofit organizations/institutions that allows
  the waiving of tipping fees.
- Initial mission assigned to the project team: Reduce the costs of
  trash removal.
- Quantify the problem in terms of cost of poor quality: The team
  developed a flowchart for the process. The costs per ton of
  trash ranged from $75 to $426. Why was there such a range in
  costs per ton?

The second stage of a diagnostic journey involves making the actual
diagnosis:

- Analyze the evidence to understand the symptoms of the
  problem: The data clearly showed that the amount of trash in
  the compactors varied considerably. In some cases compactors
  were full, and in other cases they were nearly empty.

- Redefine the mission in more precise terms based upon analysis of the symptoms: Although the team's mission could have been redefined at this point to reflect the quality of the pulls (the relative fullness of the compactor), the team decided to stay with the mission of cost reduction.

- Theorize as to what may be the cause of the symptoms: The most compelling theory had to do with scheduling of trash removal. When each new compactor was installed, a schedule was set up, but that schedule was rarely revisited or verified to ensure maximum benefit to the university. As a result, some compactors were not full when pulled.

- Arrange to test the theories to discover the cause: Arrangements were made to begin weighing the compactors. Sensory devices that would signal when a compactor was 80 percent full were installed on several compactors. Some videotaping was done at the transfer station.

- Ensure that the cause is identified and verified: The data supported the theory that compactors were being pulled too early.

The third stage involves administering the remedy:

- Develop and recommend possible remedies: A lengthy list of remedies was proposed, including changing the schedule for pulls to get closer to the 80 percent full (or greater) ideal.

- Take action to overcome resistance to remedies: Meetings were held with the contractor to discuss issues and problems. Other areas of resistance to change were explored.

- Implement the remedies: A policy of just-in-time emptying of compactors was implemented.

- Prove the adequacy of the remedies under operating conditions: Ask whether the new schedule is the best. So far, the new method is generating savings of $150,000 a year.

And the final stage involves developing a system to hold the gains:

- Ensure establishment of controls to hold the gains: The team decided to spot-check the system to ensure that sensory devices had been put into place and to monitor tonnage per compactor.

The age-old saying "We can learn more from our failures than we can from our successes" is true. There is a deep, rich form of learning embedded in the process of trying to understand what went wrong and how to do better next time. Since colleges and universities are in the learning business, we should take the saying to heart. Unfortunately, it doesn't usually work that way. As Tony's travails suggest, we tend to operate with a single-minded focus on demonstrating success. As a result of this focus, we see the critical dimension of learning as competence and the important outcome as being immediately effective. The emphasis is unwarranted. As individuals in institutions that need to improve quality and productivity, we can stand to give up some know-how to gain more know-why. Long-term effectiveness and improved performance are grounded in understanding, not just competence, and the exercise of explaining failure is a important way to gain such understanding.

Professors on a college campus regularly engage in rigorous inquiry. In their disciplinary work, they must do more than establish the events surrounding the civil rights movement or describe the RNA structure of the AIDS virus. They search for true meaning, explore cause-and-effect relationships, and develop profound understandings of complex interactions. Their most important weapon in the battle against ignorance—whether it is social injustice and disease or virtually any other issue—is the single word *why*. So, is it really too much for us to consider pursuing Tony's situation with equal vigor? Is it really too much for us to ask *why* five times until we get to a root cause? After all, if we can find a way to reduce the cost of trash removal, we should also be able to find a way to increase the chances of student success.

QUESTIONS

List several problems you are dealing with right now. What are the underlying assumptions or basic beliefs that you have concerning these problems?

Beyond the underlying assumptions, how much do you really know about the circumstances surrounding these problems?

Ask *why* five times—like peeling an onion—until you get deep into the problem.

LESSON

"Things do not exist independent of their relationship to other things."

The letter arrived on Tuesday, one week before Christmas. Paula had already received her grades for the fall semester. They were pretty good, not great, but she was a junior biology major and these were the toughest courses she would have at the college. Maybe the letter was about the research project! Her favorite professor had asked her whether she wanted to apply for a student/faculty research grant. She had jumped at the chance.

A quick rip down the side of the envelope and excitement was replaced by dismay. It was a form letter advising all sophomores and juniors of a change in housing policy. The dismay slowly turned to anger as she continued to read, "As of fall semester 1994, all college juniors and seniors will be required to live in college-owned housing." She thought of her plans. She and her friends Donna and Julie—all bio majors—were going to look for an apartment for their senior year. Anger turned to fury. What kind of bozo rule was this, anyway?

❖

Brenda stopped in mid-chew. What was her name doing in the article? She put the sandwich down on the paper plate, then pulled her chair closer to the desk. The title of the little

gem in the student newspaper was "Housing by Decree."
The subhead read, "New policy forces all students into
campus housing." There were the usual hyperbolic quotes:
"The administration treats us like kids," and "This shows
how little this school cares about students."

But right there, right on the front page, was a paragraph
about how the college's on-campus housing was only 60
percent full. The article said that estimates by the budget
director, Brenda Williams, showed that the college was
losing $250,000 in revenue each year. The article made it
sound like she was the instigator of the new policy, when all
she had done was point out the shortfall to the vice president, just as she had done last year and the year before.

❖

So much for community relations. That's all Steve Lowenthal
could think as he talked to the reporter. He'd graduated from
the college, married his zoology lab partner, and never left
town. He had built a successful electric supply business,
developed a few real estate projects, and won a seat on the
city council.

The phone had rung a few minutes before. It had been a
reporter for the local paper, someone he knew, who wanted
to know his reaction to the new college housing policy.
"What policy?" he had asked. As the reporter explained,
Steve started getting mad. Just last year he had purchased a
15-unit apartment complex five blocks from campus. He
had checked with the college's housing office before he
bought it. Freshmen and sophomores were required to live
in the dormitories. That was it. All the other numbers had
checked out, so he had dug deep into his pockets and come
up with the down payment. And now this. More than half of
his tenants were college students.

❖

The president's regular Monday morning meeting had been
expanded. In addition to the vice presidents, the director of

public affairs, the director of housing, and a few other administrators were there. Every chair around the large conference table had a body in it—all because of the new housing policy. James Bragg, the college's planning officer, had been asked by the president to attend as well.

Everybody seemed to have an opinion. It's amazing how a few phone calls from the city council and a petition signed by over a thousand students can stimulate the creative juices. There were the extremists on both ends: those who wanted the president to drop the policy and those who counseled him to do nothing, hang tough, and wait out the whiners.

What made James angry was that none of this had to happen. He had arrived in the mid-1980s to head up a strategic planning effort. One of the strategic thrusts coming out of that initial plan was to create a college district. The college's enrollment was growing steadily, but the outline of the original campus dated back to the late 1800s. They were running out of space. The idea was to expand the campus by purchasing houses adjacent to the campus, convert some to student housing and others to academic centers or offices. They bought houses and for five years they added bathrooms, fixed roofs, and applied hundreds of gallons of paint.

Trouble started in November 1990. In fact, it was November 20 at midnight, when the first complaint came in to campus police. There had been a block party organized by the students living in several of the houses. First came the kegs and the music; then the campus police arrived. It was never quite clear who threw the first punch, but the city police weren't in the mood to party. Within days the administration had written a whole new set of "get tough" regulations.

The first signs of exodus from on-campus housing occurred in the fall of the following year, and each year there were more and more empty spaces. The budget director, Brenda, had mentioned the problem. James had talked *about it, as well. He had tried to get people's attention by mentioning that some of the housing policies were probably affecting the occupancy rate and that the school had lost sight of the aim—the college district.*

But nothing ever happened. Until now, that is.

The discussion was winding down. The decision was made to appoint a policy implementation task force, charged with boosting the occupancy rate of on-campus housing while somehow placating the angry mobs.

"Brilliant," James thought. "How typical. Make the decision first, and then decide how to do it."

❖

Shelly was mad. She had only been the housing director since the summer, but this was not her first job. Before she moved here she was the housing director at another school for almost 10 years, so she knew something about housing.

The vice president for business, her boss, had staff meetings every Tuesday morning. It was during her second or third meeting that the budget director had given the now-infamous occupancy rate report. The trend line that Brenda Williams drew was nearly perfect. Beginning in 1991, the rates had gone from 90 percent to 75 percent to 60 percent in three years. Brenda had punctuated her graph by calculating what the 30 percent drop meant in terms of lost revenues. The quarter of a million dollars had gotten the vice president's attention. From that point on, things had been on the "new policy" fast track.

Over the past few weeks, Shelly had done her own informal marketing research. There were some definite advantages to living on campus; for example, the walk to classes was much shorter and the college was really good about responding to problems like leaky faucets. The drawbacks, however, were obvious to anyone—like a college junior—who was willing to shop around. Living on campus was more expensive—not a lot, but enough to make a difference. Then there were the rules: no pets, no opposite-sex

*housemates, no loud music past 7:00 P.M. during the week
and 10:00 P.M. on the weekends, no non-student stay-overs
without written permission . . . the list of "no's" filled two
pages.*
   *Shelly didn't want or need the new policy. And she didn't
want or need the vice president telling her how to do her job.*

❖❖❖

It has probably been some time since you purchased a gumball, but
think back to the process. You put a coin into the slot and crank a
handle, a gumball in the bottom of the glass bowl slides down a chute,
then you pull the metal flap back and get it—usually a color that you
don't want. Your attention is probably on the gumball you are getting,
not on the other hundred or so that remain behind, but what do you
think happens to them while your gumball is sliding down the chute?

The removal of a gumball triggers a series of adjustments. The relationship that each remaining gumball has with those around it changes.
The disruption is undoubtedly greatest near the bottom of the bowl.
Nonetheless, the interdependence of the gumballs is such that a transformation resonates throughout the glass bowl. In fact, try to remove
one without disturbing the rest (make sure you bring a lot of coins).

If gumballs do not exist independent of their relationships with other
gumballs in a glass bowl, does the same conclusion hold true for people
and events in organizations? Many organizational researchers believe
so; few organizational practitioners behave so.

In her excitingly eclectic book *Leadership and the New Science: Learning about Organization from an Orderly Universe*, Margaret Wheatley suggests that scientists in many different disciplines are questioning
whether we can adequately explain how the world works by using the
machine imagery created by Sir Isaac Newton and others in the seven-
teenth century.[1] The assumption behind the machine model is that we
can understand the system, or the whole, by comprehending the workings of the parts. According to this model, the world is characterized
by materialism and reductionism.

Most of today's organizations, according to Wheatley, are Newtonian. "Responsibilities have been organized into functions," she says. "People have been organized into roles. Page after page of organizational charts depict the workings of the machine: the number of pieces, what fits where, who the big pieces are."[2] We reduce, describe, and separate things. We make boxes and establish inviolate boundaries. Then we make rules to reinforce the hard edges and develop job descriptions that further chunk up the work processes and systems into pieces. Communication and connectedness are discouraged through the use of function-specific lexicon and policies.

Colleges and universities have all the characteristics of a nicely dissected Newtonian organization. We have organizational charts in which we distinguish between administrative, academic, and student functions. We build layers—department chairs, deans and directors, vice presidents, and provosts. Our most glorious testimony to machine imagery is, of course, the curriculum. We distinguish between general education (lower division) and the major (upper division) and proceed to serve up learning in neat little courses chosen from a catalog. If students successfully negotiate 40 or so, they are admitted into the community of scholars.

The nonsystemic orientation of Newtonian organizations, colleges and universities included, produces a broad array of dysfunctions. Peter Senge, the systems theorist, refers to these as learning disabilities. He describes seven in *The Fifth Discipline*, but I will limit my discussion to four that are well illustrated in our story.[3] The first relevant learning disability is "I am my position," which suggests that when people in organizations focus only on their positions they feel little sense of responsibility for results produced by the system. Moreover, when results are disappointing, it is usually difficult to establish causality. The best we can do is assume that "someone screwed up."

One of the first impressions we get from the story is everyone was doing his or her job. Brenda, the budget director, crunched the numbers like she was supposed to. James, the planning officer, developed a strategic plan just as his job description said he should. Early on, the president and others exercised "get tough" regulations to keep the housing situation from getting out of control. Finally, the vice president for business took his fiduciary responsibility seriously and protected the school's assets by issuing the new housing policy. So, if everyone was doing things right, why the mess? Why is everyone so mad? Part of the answer lies in the way the college sliced and diced the process of providing housing for its primary customers—the students. Everyone had a piece of the action—the strategic issues, the financial reports, the policies and procedures—but no one was responsible for seeing how the pieces interacted (the subject of lesson 3, on unattended work processes).

A second learning disability, "The enemy is out there," is a by-product of "I am my position." When we focus only on our positions, our organizational pigeonholes, we do not see how our actions extend beyond the boundaries of those positions. When our actions have negative consequences, we assume that the source of the problems must lie elsewhere. It is, of course, easy to dismiss any responsibility for an outcome if our contributions were limited to a narrow slice of the process. Why should we take the rap?

Brenda's reaction makes sense. She just noted the budget shortfall to the vice president; she didn't purchase the properties and didn't attend the now-legendary party. James's reaction makes sense as well. He knows the problem is not his fault. After all, he told the administrators the housing policies were probably affecting occupancy rates, but no one listened to him. Shelly, the housing director, is new to her job, but in this baptism by fire she's getting the hang of things. She's absolutely certain the problem is the vice president, who is intruding into her area, her position.

Another learning disability, according to Senge, is a "fixation on events." One tenet of a reductionist philosophy is that any discrete part is a representation of the whole: if we can understand the human cell, we can understand the human. Such a philosophy results in a society and organizations that are fixated on short-term events. We report crime, but we don't seek to understand the causes of crime; we look to quarterly reports, but we don't actively manage the new product development process; we have tenure decisions, but we don't have highly evolved methods for improving teaching. Our attention is devoted to the event, not to what came before it or after it. The result, according to Senge, is that we are often distracted from seeing the long-term patterns of change that lie behind the events and from understanding the causes of those patterns. The events that dominate our story are the November 20, 1990, party and the student petition. They stand out in bold relief. The methodical development of the strategic plan and the slow erosion of on-campus occupancy simply did not inspire the same kind of attention.

The last learning disability, "the illusion of taking charge," is a fitting finale to the previous three. Each person views a set of events from his or her own organizational pigeonhole. Each is convinced that he or she is not responsible; the enemy is elsewhere. Into this mix stir a norm that says we value action and decisiveness in our leadership. (Indeed, when was the last time you remember someone being rewarded for raising difficult questions about current policies rather than solving urgent problems?) The result is the thoroughly modern, tough decision maker. Unfortunately, as Senge points out, such proactiveness is often nothing more than reactiveness in disguise.

Our story is illustrative. First there was the stimulus (the party), then the response (a whole new set of "get tough" regulations). Although the administrators in the story probably perceived themselves as decisive, they merely reacted to an event. Their decisions, in turn, set in motion a series of reactions. The nature of this transformed environment was made manifest in the budget director's declining numbers. The second stimulus kicked in when the vice president decided that the numbers were no longer acceptable. His position, chief financial officer, demanded a response to this new turn of events. Using the same "take charge" mentality, he did what he had to do and issued the new thou-shalt-live-on-campus edict.

The players in our little drama are either unaware of or unimpressed by the gumball analogy. Their "I am my position" perspective suggests that they see people and events as independent. It follows, then, that when an event occurs—say, a disruptive party—their reaction is to take charge, be decisive. They are fixated on the event, not on the chain reaction their decisions set off. When the gumball was removed, the glass bowl was transformed through a series of rearrangements as the other gumballs adjusted to the new circumstances. When each of the housing policies was issued, it too created a chain reaction based on the interdependence of people in the system. Because they do not address this interdependence, the administration's actions resemble those of a drunk walking home. A general direction is set, followed by a series of faltering steps. Each misstep provokes a delayed overreaction in the other direction. The result is a zigzag path, characterized by bumps and bruises and intermittent statements attesting to sobriety and the ability to make it home unscathed. The administration gets there late, if at all, and pays for its reactive approach with a splitting headache.[4]

Wheatley, Senge, and others argue that reductionist thinking no longer works. What is needed, instead, is an approach that shifts our focus from events to interdependence, from parts and pieces to systems and wholes. Wheatley, in her work, explores the nature of quantum mechanics, in which scientists have observed a level of connectedness among seemingly discrete parts widely separated in time and space. In this subatomic world, relationships are the key determinants of what is observed. Reality is not so much "things" as the pattern that connects the "things." To live in a quantum world, Wheatley suggests:

> We will need to stop describing tasks and instead facilitate process. We will need to become savvy about how to build relationships, how to nurture growing, evolving things. All of us will need better skills in listening, communicating, and facilitating groups, because these are the talents that build strong relationships. . . . The quantum world has demolished the concept of the unconnected individual.[5]

The quantum world is one in which the myopic search for trees is less important than the panoramic view of the forest. It is a world less and less defined by boundaries and more and more defined by inter-dependencies. The focus is on the connection between all the gumballs that make up a complex system—not on any particular gumball, iso-lated and separated from the others.

Several colleges and universities are attempting to take a systems approach to their work. Key faculty, staff, and administrators at Jack-son Community College in Michigan, for example, have considered the question "How does work get done?" in an attempt to understand their organization as a system. That question led to others: "Who are our customers and what are their needs?" "What are our products and services?" "How do we know whether our products and services are any good?" "What are our expected outcomes and results?" "What sys-tems produce our products and services?" "What resources are required to operate the systems?" By answering these questions, Jackson Com-munity College developed a system map that enabled faculty, staff, and administrators to see the whole, not just the parts. A series of team projects directed at making fundamental changes in the way the work is done has followed. As Clyde LeTarte, the president of Jackson, stated, "While fire-fighting is still a necessary evil, recognition for superior management will go to those who understand systems thinking, who manage complex systems effectively and who implement systemic im-provements, not just quick solutions."[6]

The administration at the University of Tampa has relegated the industrial-based organizational structure, which was in place on its cam-pus as well as on those of the overwhelming majority of other institu-tions, to the trash heap of history.[7] According to Tampa's president, David Ruffer, the structure doesn't work in an information/service en-vironment. He and a core group of campus innovators have set out to redesign their working relationships. The driving force behind the re-design is the perceived need to improve work processes, not the con-trol of functions. To that end, the redesigned structure has only two divisions: the educational enterprise and the economic enterprise. Within these enterprises, efforts are underway to identify key work processes and involve those people who can best address those processes in the continuous improvement of services to constituents. In effect, a systems view of the institution has become the starting point, the foundation for designing and managing a university that can respond more effectively to the reality of a service environment.

Members of the George Mason University community experienced the same desire to change the way in which work is managed by forming a working group on service improvement. They decided to take a systems approach to the redesign of work processes that span many units. The initial emphasis has been on three areas: curriculum management, research and development management, and payroll and personnel actions. GMU's general methodology reflects a quantum world perspective in which relationships are the key to understanding. First, they form a task force to investigate a process, then task force members map the existing process using loop notation (a tool used by systems thinkers).[8] The idea is to study interrelationships rather than linear cause-and-effect chains, and to see processes of change rather than static snapshots.

The lesson I have tried to illustrate—"Things do not exist independent of their relationship to other things."—goes to the heart of many of the quality and productivity problems we experience in our Newtonian institutions. The gumball analogy may not impress you; it evokes silly, childhood images. The problems that our colleges and universities are facing, however, are anything but silly. They, like our drunk, stumble back and forth, fighting one crisis while unconsciously sowing the seeds of the next crisis. There is a better way. We need to adjust our focus so that the organizational parts fade into the background and the whole—the system—emerges as the primary unit of analysis.

QUESTIONS

What is your primary unit of analysis? Do you think in parts, or do you think in wholes?

Review the major problems or issues facing your institution. Can they be solved through piecemeal, analytic approaches?

What are some of the behaviors that a holistic thinker would exhibit? How would they contrast with the behaviors of a reductionist thinker?

How would you begin to take a holistic approach to issues at your institution?

PART 5

PERSONAL INVOLVEMENT

PERFORMANCE IMPROVEMENT FRAMEWORK

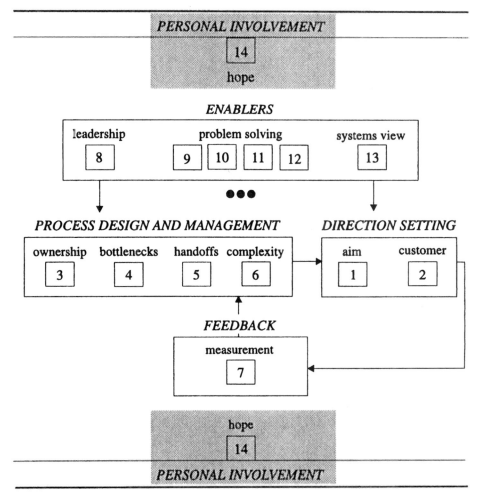

LESSON 14

"Spread hope."

Terry took the call in the warehouse. "Terry, this is Lynn over in student services. I just heard. I took last week off—went to the mountains. How are you guys doing?" Terry sat down on the corner of the desk. "We're okay, a bit singed around the edges, but we're doing all right."

"How'd it happen?"

"Well, they were putting on a new roof over the weekend. The hot tar overflowed and the building caught on fire," he explained.

"What's left? Did they save anything?"

"Not much," he replied. "One of the copiers is still working, but the presses, the mailing machines—it was pretty much a total meltdown. And what the fire didn't get, the water did."

Lynn went on, saying how sorry she was. Terry had gotten dozens of such calls since the fire. It was like a family member had died. Just before she hung up, though, Lynn added, "You know, I thought they were kidding me this morning when my secretary mentioned the fire. Some new fellow, said his name was Tom, came by. He dropped off mail, picked up mail, and not a word. How are you managing?"

"I don't know how," he responded. "But we are."

Terry hung up the phone and looked through the doorway out into the warehouse. How were they doing it? Some local companies were helping with the copying and two "loaners" had arrived last week. Another state university had volunteered to cover some of the printing. They had relocated in a warehouse and set up a makeshift mail service. Still, it was mid-June and about 100° out there. No ventilation. Lousy lighting. This was the sixth straight day of double shifts for some of them, yet, as Lynn had mentioned, if it hadn't been for the burned-out hulk of a building on the edge of campus, most people wouldn't have known anything had happened. They had barely skipped a beat.

And they had done most of it on their own. The mailroom crew put together its own overtime schedule. The copy machine operators formed a water damage team. Two inventory clerks, Tom was one, were delivering mail.

God, Terry was proud of these people.

❖

Terry had been at the university for almost 30 years. He had started out in the physical plant, but for the last 10 years he had been director of printing and mailing services. He learned his own management philosophy from his boss, "Don't screw up and I won't bother you." Perhaps that explained why Terry had worked in the physical plant for four years before he had gotten his first performance review. Then a new vice president arrived, and Terry's world changed.

Jessica was a believer. She believed they could do better. She believed in concepts like teamwork and open communications, and she acted on those beliefs. There was a new emphasis on training, problem-solving tools, and leadership skills. Resources were devoted to project-based improvement efforts.

At first Terry was hesitant—he'd been there for a long time, and he knew how things were done. After several months, however, Terry became a believer. He could trace his conversion to the week the president announced budget cuts. Jessica put all 11 directors in a room and announced, "We're going to work on the budget." As a group, they worked through it. There was some blood on the floor at the end, but everyone was invigorated by the fact that they were involved in the process, their voices were heard, their opinions were valued, and the solution (however painful) was theirs.

Over the next two years things really took off. Word had gotten out about the training, and a few of Terry's people asked whether they could go. Afterward, they came to him with a project idea—to reduce the turnaround time on bulk mail. He facilitated the group. The project was hard work, but interesting and great fun. They cut the time in half. Jessica, the vice president, asked the team to make a presentation to the other directors. Then another team formed and another. It was like an epidemic of enthusiasm. People started thinking, they started asking tough questions, and they started talking to each other. The department was a different place. You could almost taste the difference.

Then the fire.

❖

Terry walked out into the warehouse. It was 5:00 but no one showed any signs of leaving. He kept thinking back to the budget crisis two years earlier and how they had come through it. Initially, there was such fear; everyone was thinking about themselves—their jobs, their departments. But afterward, after the information had been shared, the problems discussed openly and honestly, and a rational approach to consensus building used, the fear had given way to hope. Maybe they could influence events and shape their own environments. Two years of personal change and

*nurturing the same approach with his department had been
the most satisfying of his life.*

*Terry hadn't been sure how successful he had been. He
didn't know whether he, or the people he worked with, had
changed—really changed—until now.*

❖❖❖

The scenario being played out on a Monday afternoon in an oven-
hot warehouse is not typical of most work environments. Sure, in a
time of crisis people will rally together and do some extra work. As a
general rule, though, most people do not get excited about work; they
get excited about their life outside of work. They care about their pay-
checks, their vacations, and their kids' baseball games. They do what
they have to do and not much more. After a while there is no spark in
their eyes, no hop in their step. Everything is seen to be something
extra, so the primary motivating forces used to change or improve
things are carrots and sticks.

So, how do you explain the response to the fire? No bribes are being
offered and no "Let's win this one for the Gipper" speeches are being
made. People are responding to a difficult situation with initiative, emotion, and personal pride. They are not waiting to be told what to do,
and they are not making excuses or whining. They seem to care genu-
inely about their work and about each other. You get the feeling that
no matter what happens, this crew believes it can handle it. Hope is in
the air; even if the air is stale and heated to a toasty 100°.

Do not make the mistake, however, of confusing the situation in the
warehouse with some sort of "group hug," a cutesy slogan on a wall
poster, or something you might learn in a personal development semi-
nar. The kind of hope that is flourishing under the difficult conditions
in the story is a bone-deep belief system based on a unique combination of attitudes and behaviors, supplemented by tangible outcomes.
Hope is real.

The initial component of this belief system is personal involvement.
An entertaining and insightful way of understanding the concept of

involvement is the subject of *Zapp! The Lightning Power of Empowerment* by William Byham and Jeff Cox.[1] The book is a modern-day fable set in a large company with many departments. At the center of the fable is a technician, Ralph, who invents a machine (a Ralpholater) that enables him to walk around the company in the 12th dimension. In the 12th dimension, other people cannot see him and Ralph is able to see a light surrounding people and their interactions with others that is a measure of creative energy, responsibility, and knowledge. In his wanderings around the company, one of the first things Ralph realizes is how dull and dark his own department (Department N) is and how energized Department Z is. He can't figure it out. Department Z is doing regular work, nothing special or particularly interesting, but " . . . nobody seemed bored here. It looked just like every other office. And yet there was something different in the air. The people here were so *involved* in what they were doing—whatever it was." A little while later Ralph reflected on what he had seen, "People moved with purpose. They worked with purpose. There was a quiet hustle and bustle throughout the place."[2]

Building a belief system in which improvement is not only possible but expected begins with a behavior—involving people in such fundamental aspects of their work as the exchange of information and collaborative decision making. This behavior is the sharing of power. The personal involvement witnessed in the fictitious world of the Ralpholater is the same force, the same "zapp," that Terry felt two years ago when he and the other directors were asked to help solve a budget problem. He was zapped again when he went through training, and again when his project team's efforts to improve were recognized.

The act of involving people in all aspects of work life that affect them is where improvement starts. Such a change is not easy; indeed, it may very well be impossible for some. Letting go is often the most difficult step toward improving performance. Sharing power—responsibility, leadership, information—threatens the self-image and status of many administrators and managers. Nonetheless, if the behavior is not there, if the act of sharing power is not forthcoming, the notion of improvement will reside only in the exhortations of supervisors, not in the hearts and minds of individuals.

The second part of a belief system that spreads hope is the attitude that results from the act of pursuing personal involvement and sharing power—a feeling of self-determination. We are most likely to be enthusiastic about what we are doing and to do it well when we are free to make decisions about the way we carry out a task. To describe much of what is wrong with our workplaces is to enumerate the effects of restricting people's sense of self-determination. Control stifles choice and results in sameness, mediocrity, and reactivity. Having choices sets people free.

Sharing power through involvement creates a profound feeling of self-determination, an attitude that is palpable in the actions of Terry's crew. Terry isn't forcing anyone to work overtime or shift jobs; he didn't make promises or threats. The individuals are doing what they think is necessary to respond to the situation. Their attitude about their work has changed because, in the words of Byham and Cox, they have been zapped, not sapped:

When you have been sapped, you feel like . . .
  Your job belongs to the company.
  You are just doing whatever you are told.
  Your job doesn't really matter.
  You don't know how well you're doing.
  You always have to keep your mouth shut.
  Your job is something different from who your are.
  You have little or no control over your work.

When you are zapped, you feel like . . .
  Your job belongs to you.
  You are responsible.
  Your job counts for something.
  You know where you stand.
  You have some say in how things are done.
  Your job is a part of who you are.
  You have some control over your work.[3]

The third component of the belief system is the outcome—performance improvement. Allowing people to manage their work and solve their own problems, coupled with a strong sense of vision and purpose, provides a powerful motivator that improves performance. This conclusion is not the stuff of fables; the evidence is clear. According to a broad array of research studies, the greater the level of personal involvement, the greater the payoff.[4] The quality of the product or service is improved, better decisions are made, and employee retention increases when people are encouraged to question, to learn, to think, and to grow. Terry, our manager, does not need to review the results of these or any other studies. He does not need to understand the research designs, the data gathering and analyses, or the interpretations. The people who work in his department know all about improvement, about doing things better, faster, and cheaper. Improvement is what they have been doing, as part of their everyday work life and in their team projects, for the last two years.

The final piece to the puzzle is another attitude—personal satisfaction. Many people, especially managers, are under the mistaken impression that performance is a function of happiness. The result is a management philosophy based upon rewards, prizes, back-slapping, and a host of other incentives. Organizations have service awards, employee-of-the-month awards, "dress down" days, and catered birthday parties, all designed to promote happiness. A happy employee is a productive employee, right? Not necessarily. Rewards induce the same behavior as punishments—that is, compliance. When bribed, people do what they are bribed to do, nothing more. Management-by-reward does not generally alter the attitudes and emotional commitment that underlie behaviors; it merely uses a treat (a bone) to induce an act (a bark).

While there is solid evidence to link personal involvement (being zapped) with performance, there is little evidence to indicate that employee satisfaction has any lasting cause-and-effect relationship with performance.[5] So, happiness is unimportant? Hardly. Personal satisfaction still has a key link to performance, but not as a cause. Satisfaction is an effect. Performance improvement, driven by involvement and self-determination, leads to higher personal satisfaction rather than the other way around. People get a kick out of improving their work; they want to do well. All they ask is that they be given a voice in setting the goals, that they have access to the necessary tools and information, and that leaders work hard to remove the barriers that keep them from doing their best work.

The belief system just described, one that spreads hope, is a composite of attitudes, behaviors, and results. The system operates as a reinforcing loop: the greater the personal involvement, the more self-determination, the better the job performance, the more personal satisfaction, the greater the personal involvement. . . . Taken in its entirety, the belief system—indeed, this entire book—is a testimony to the reinforcing power of intrinsic motivation. The desire to do something and do it well simply cannot be imposed; it comes from within. Administrators and supervisors do not motivate people by giving them big raises or new status symbols—a corner office, a slick title. Rather, people are motivated by their inherent need to succeed at a challenging task. Management's job, it follows, is not to motivate people so that they will achieve; instead, management should seek out opportunities for people to achieve so they will become motivated—zapped, if you will.[6]

Refer back to this book's organizing scheme and its component parts: direction setting, process design and management, feedback, and enablers. What would be the effect of involving people in each of these activities? Wouldn't they develop a sense of self-determination which, in turn, would impact performance? Wouldn't they, then, become motivated and experience joy in work? Don't the other 13 lessons constitute a belief system that spreads hope? Take direction setting. People are most motivated when they are able to participate in making decisions about organizational or unit aims. Through involvement, they come to know what is important, why it is important, and why their own work is important. Many of the most successful organizations are built on this principle. They know that top-down direction setting may yield compliance but never commitment. A powerful shared vision is rooted in personal visions.

A similar effect can be observed when people are involved in process design. In the last few years many books have been published on process design and management (some were cited in earlier lessons). Two messages are embedded in these books:

1. Quality can be designed into processes and systems
2. The people who need to be intimately involved in the design and redesign of processes and systems are the people who are actually doing the work

In effect, the people who work in the process should work on the process. To do otherwise, to rob people of the direct responsibility for creating and improving their own environment, is the ultimate source of control and the greatest demoralizer of all.

Feedback, the next component, is the key learning loop in the framework. As we have seen, feedback functions best when used to provide simple, straightforward, and valuable information about how well someone or something is doing. The information is then used to modify processes, policies, behaviors, and, in some cases, the aim. If the people who work in a process being monitored are not involved in determining the nature of the feedback, however, the emphasis of the exercise necessarily shifts from improvement to accountability. People interpret feedback as something that is being done to them, not for them, and their interpretation is absolutely correct. Whereas feedback without involvement is a control device—a great big sap—feedback with involvement is a lightning bolt of learning, growth, and self-determination.

Finally, in the introduction enablers were described as a "critical influence on the rate at which the organization creates the knowledge required to alter its practices." Most of the lessons in the enabler section of the book discuss problem-solving approaches that work to enhance organizational learning and, consequently, improve performance. By training people in these approaches, then encouraging them to use problem-solving methods in their work, you *enable* them to effect change. No longer do they have to just respond to problems or complaints; they can challenge assumptions, generate information, and think through options. They can create opportunities and pursue their own ideas. They have the power of choice. If capable, well-trained people are placed in a setting with clear expectations, minimal interference, reinforcing consequences, and appropriate feedback, they will be motivated. They will find joy in work.

A useful illustration of this lesson is the experience of the Department of Human Resources (HR) at Oregon State University (OSU). The university, and its human resources director Jacquelyn Rudolph, have been pursuing a quality agenda for years. The HR staff has been trained in quality management tools. Staff members practice job rotation, work in teams, and are encouraged to look for improvement opportunities. They are deeply involved.

One headache that never seemed to go away, however, was the system for recruiting and hiring for classified positions. The process was a standard one run by the personnel division of the state of Oregon for 40,000 positions in the state—one standard posting practice, one standard application, one standard test. "It just didn't suit our needs," is how the director put it. "It was tuned into the central Oregon region. We're 45 miles south of Salem—off the beaten path. We were convinced that the test was not a valid predictor of success for us. And it took six to eight weeks to get a test score." For a department trying to fill a position, the process was very discouraging. The department would eventually get three or four lists with the names of 30 applicants, but by the time the lists arrived most applicants, especially the good people who were qualified and wanted to work, had already taken jobs. Many others lived around Salem and did not want to drive to Corvallis.

The sheer frustration of being victimized on a daily basis by a bad system drove a group of HR staff people to the director, asking her to approach the state personnel division about the possibility of OSU's working on the problem. Rudolph's response was, "I am willing to do this. I am willing to run interference. But you need to understand that it will be a real fluid environment. This will mean adversity—and you

don't have to do it. It's your call." The group met, convinced themselves of the technical necessity of pursuing the project, and then returned: "We're ready to go."

After months of negotiating and haggling, Rudolph was able to convince the state to allow OSU to "decouple" for a one-year period. "We
wanted to challenge the whole methodology, so we asked to form a
partnership with the state. We agreed to feed them data, document
what we did, and measure our performance; they agreed to cut us loose
and reevaluate the situation in a year." The year was both exhilarating
and exhausting. The HR staff members developed a whole new front-
end process to screen applicants and make a better match between the
applicant and the position. They reduced the turnaround time on the
test and distribution of the list of qualified applicants from six to eight
weeks to three days. Now the departments get just one list with five
names of people who are willing and qualified to work.

The experiment has been so successful that the state is considering a
certification process that would allow other agencies to do what OSU
did. Understandably, the HR crew is proud of its efforts, which, according to Rudolph, ". . . just came out of a need to express what our
real needs were and not put us in a sort of vanilla-colored grouping
and say, 'live with it.' " It also came out of Jacquelyn Rudolph's ability
to share power, involve people, and make work joyful.

From the tone of this chapter, the points made, and the OSU illustration, the reader might conclude that this lesson only applies to industry or the administrative side of the academic enterprise. After all,
the critical process of a college or university—teaching and learning—
centers on people who are by definition involved in their work, professors who are committed to doing an excellent job in the classroom and
students who appreciate the importance of an education. There are
numerous examples of such dynamic interactions every day on college
campuses across the country; nonetheless, there is every reason to believe that some serious zapping might be beneficial to the teaching
and learning process. Indeed, the list of sapped feelings enumerated
earlier bears a scary resemblance to the classroom experiences of many

college students: "You are just doing whatever you are told," "You don't know how well you are doing," and "You have little or no control over your work."

In lesson 2—"Left to our own devices, we pay too much attention to things of too little importance to the customer."—I described the work of several Miami University professors, Gary Shulman and David Luechauer, who were pursuing an "empowered learner" approach to their classes. The emphasis was on creating a collaborative environment where "students have the opportunity to shape the nature of their work." Although Miami's student-as-partner approach is innovative and refreshing, it is encouraging to know that this is not an isolated incident. Personal involvement in the classroom, along with the idea that enabling students to influence their environment has a direct effect on their willingness and ability to perform, is a zapp that is long overdue on most campuses.

For example, in a Money and Banking course at Central Missouri State University, the professor, George Wilson, expects students to help develop the expected outcomes for the class. While introducing other basic materials, he spends the first two weeks facilitating the work of small teams of students who attempt to answer the question "What do we need to learn in this class?" by interviewing employers as well as professors of several next-in-line courses. According to Wilson, "There is always some fumbling around initially—they've never had to do anything like this—but there is a lot of learning in terms of why we do particular things and why other things are important." Teams of students also work on determining how the class is going to demonstrate the competencies. The result is a set of corresponding learning levels. Further, the students devise their own set of performance measures— e.g., exams, individual and group homework assignments, class quizzes, short essays, and oral/visual presentations. "I teach fewer things but I teach them better," Wilson says. "And the students spend more time on assignments—working with each other and redoing things they are not pleased with."

Down in Texas, at Richland College, another professor, Gary John, teaches a sophomore literature course with three other professors. They begin the course by organizing the class into teams. The student teams are then assigned to different parts of the globe—Africa, Australia, Asia—and given the task of identifying a mix of current authors. The teams examine book reviews and consult with professors and editors before submitting their recommendations. A consensus results in a final list of readings. The professors also involve the students in the grading process. Students are given a lecture on feedback—its importance and how to do it effectively—then they are expected to read each other's papers. Rewrites are much encouraged. John says, "The level of preparation for each class is phenomenal. And the biggest question from the students, at the end of the course, is: 'What other courses at the college are taught this way?' "

It does not seem to matter whether the scene is a temporary mailroom set up in a warehouse or a literature class at a small college in Dallas, Texas. Inspired performances are not something that can be bought or bartered. Threatening people, badgering them, humiliating them, or weighing them down under a heavy burden of accountability can produce some short-term gains, but only at the cost of long-term resentment and bitterness. The real key to unlocking improved quality and productivity in an organization is embedded in a belief system that begins with the act of relinquishing control and involving people in the important aspects of their own work. This simple act results in a profound sense of self-determination. Such personal ownership and the accompanying power of choice become the driving forces behind a commitment to reflect and sacrifice, to stretch and grow, to aim high and work smart, and to improve their own performance continuously. It is an incredibly satisfying journey for people, one that is joyful, one that spreads hope.

QUESTIONS

What kind of investment has the institution made in increasing the ability of people to make their own best decisions?

In what ways has the institution tried to minimize control and maximize responsibility?

What specific steps have you taken, or could you take, to increase the level of personal involvement that those around you experience in their work?

NOTES

LESSON 1

"Begin with the end in mind."

1. This story is adapted with permission from the chapter "Kidgets," by Maury Cotter and Daniel Seymour, in *Kidgets and Other Insightful Stories about Quality in Education* (Milwaukee, WI: American Society for Quality Control, 1993).
2. Susan Ferriss and Libby Lewis, "Stanford Reinstates Failing Grades," *San Francisco Examiner*, June 3, 1994, A-1.
3. W. Edwards Deming, *Out of the Crisis* (Cambridge, MA: Massachusetts Institute of Technology Center for Advanced Engineering Study, 1982).
4. Peter M. Senge, *The Fifth Discipline* (New York: Doubleday, 1990).
5. Steven R. Covey, *Principle-Centered Leadership* (New York: Summit Books, 1991).

LESSON 2

"Left to our own devices, we pay too much attention to things of too little importance to the customer."

1. The Malcolm Baldrige National Quality Award is managed by the National Institute of Standards and Technology (NIST). Copies of each year's award criteria are available at the following address: NIST, Route 270 and Quince Orchard Road, Administration Building, Room A537, Gaithersburg, MD 20899-0001. In 1995, education and health care categories will be tested with awards tentatively scheduled for 1996. See also, Daniel Seymour "The Baldrige Cometh," *Change* 26, no. 1 (January–February 1994): 16–27.

2. For an example of how G. Clotaire Rapaille's work relates to quality management, see Marilyn R. Zuckerman and Lewis J. Hatala, *Incredibly American: Releasing the Heart of Quality* (Milwaukee, WI: American Society for Quality Control, 1992).

3. One study that looks at the effects of language in the implementation of quality management in higher education is Daniel Seymour, *Clearing the Hurdles: A Survey on Strategies for Implementing Quality Management Practices in Higher Education* (Methuen, MA: GOAL/QPC, 1993).

4. Joseph M. Juran, *Juran on Planning for Quality* (New York: The Free Press, 1988).

5. Michael Hammer and James Champy, *Reengineering the Corporation* (New York: HarperCollins, 1993), 130.

6. Thomas H. Davenport, *Process Innovation: Reengineering Work through Information Technology* (Boston, MA: Harvard Business School Press, 1993), 15.

7. For a more detailed description, see Gary M. Shulman and David L. Luechauer, "The Empowering Educator: A CQI Approach to Classroom Leadership," in *Continuous Quality Improvement: Making the Transition to Education* edited by Dean L. Hubbard (Marysville, MO: Prescott Publishing, 1993), 424–53.

LESSON 3

"Waste is the unintended consequence of unattended work processes."

1. Value analysis is an important aspect of continuous quality improvement that receives scant attention in education. Two references are worth reviewing. Joseph M. Juran discusses value analysis in *Juran on Planning for Quality* (New York: The Free Press, 1988). A related perspective, the value chain, forms the basis for Michael E. Porter's *Competitive Advantage: Creating and Sustaining Superior Performance* (New York: The Free Press, 1985). While both authors are primarily interested in industry and corresponding issues, value is an increasingly important concept in higher education in light of our seeming inability to control costs.

2. H. James Harrington, *Business Process Improvement* (New York: McGraw-Hill, 1991), 5.

3. Adapted from Geary A. Rummler and Alan P. Brache, *Improving Performance: How to Manage the White Space on the Organization Chart* (San Francisco, CA: Jossey-Bass, 1990), 134.

4. For additional information regarding Xavier's model, contact Professor Helmut Roehrig, Chairman, Department of Music, Xavier University, Cincinnati, OH 45207, or Samuel C. Welch, Director, Xavier University Opera Workshop, P.O. Box 55, Cincinnati, OH 45201-0055.

LESSON 4

"The capacity of a system is limited by its bottlenecks."

1. Eliyahu M. Goldratt, *The Goal* (Croton-on-Hudson, NY: North River Press, 1992).
2. These data are taken from two 1993 California Higher Education Policy Center reports: *On the Brink*, by Jack McCurdy and William Trombley, and *By Design or Default*, by Patrick M. Callan and Joni E. Finney (San Jose, CA: California Higher Education Policy Center, 1993).
3. Patrick M. Callan and Joni E. Finney, *By Design or Default* (San Jose, CA: California Higher Education Policy Center, 1993), i.
4. See, for example, Daniel Seymour, "A Discriminant Analysis of Early Retirees in Academe," Southern Marketing Association Proceedings, Orlando, FL, November 1985.
5. For an excellent discussion of the productivity of learning, please see D. Bruce Johnstone, "Enhancing the Productivity of Learning," *AAHE Bulletin* 46, no. 4 (December 1993). The issue also contains the reactions of six educators to Johnstone's propositions.
6. This idea, along with its counterpart, which follows in the text, is discussed in *The Goal* on pages 158–59 and 233. A closely related concept is known as load smoothing. A discussion of load smoothing can be found in Alan Robinson (ed.), *Continuous Improvement in Operations: A Systematic Approach to Waste Reduction* (Cambridge, MA: Productivity Press, 1991), 73–86.

LESSON 5

"An organization is a relay team; the better the handoffs, the better the results."

1. W. Edwards Deming, *Out of the Crisis* (Cambridge, MA: Massachusetts Institute of Technology Center for Advanced Engineering Study, 1982).
2. Howard S. Gitlow and Shelly J. Gitlow, *The Deming Guide to Quality and Competitive Position* (Englewood Cliffs, NJ: Prentice-Hall, 1987).
3. William F. Massy, Andrea K. Wilger, and Carol Colbeck, "Overcoming 'Hollowed' Collegiality," *Change* 26, no. 4 (July–August 1994): 11–20.
4. For further information on a tool that can help generate the "voice of the customer," see Stan Marsh et al., *Quality Function Deployment* (Methuen, MA: GOAL/QPC, 1991). A higher education application is the subject of an article by Burt Peachy and Daniel Seymour, "Voice of the Customer: Using QFD as a Strategic Planning Tool," in *Continuous Quality Improvement: Making the Transition to Education* edited by Dean L. Hubbard (Maryville, OH: Prescott Publishing, 1993).
5. The work of this team has been facilitated by Michael Dooris, a research and planning associate at Pennsylvania State University. Some of his experiences

with the team are described in "A Planner Studies Physics," *Planning for Higher Education* 21 (Summer 1993): 1–8.
6. See Geary A. Rummler and Alan P. Brache, *Improving Performance: How to Manage the White Space on the Organization Chart* (San Francisco, CA: Jossey-Bass, 1990), 135.

LESSON 6

"In the absence of a search for the unnecessary, complexity drives out simplicity."

1. These works include: William F. Massy and Robert Zemsky, "Faculty Discretionary Time: Departments and the Academic Ratchet," in *Policy Perspectives* (Philadelphia, PA: The Pew Higher Education Research Program, 1992); Robert Zemsky, "Curriculum and Cost: Notes on the Utilization of Teaching Resources," *Liberal Education* 76, no. 4 (September–October 1990): 26–30; Robert Zemsky, *Structure and Coherence: Measuring the Undergraduate Curriculum* (Washington, DC: Association of American Colleges, 1989).
2. Peter R. Scholtes, *The Team Handbook* (Madison, WI: Joiner Associates, 1988).
3. The value chain concept forms much of the basis for the notion of competitive advantage as described by Michael E. Porter in his book *Competitive Advantage: Creating and Sustaining Superior Performance* (New York: The Free Press, 1985). See chapter 2 of the book.
4. A thorough description of this subject is found in H. James Harrington, *Business Process Improvement: The Breakthrough Strategy for Total Quality, Productivity, and Competitiveness* (New York: McGraw-Hill, 1991). See chapter 6 of the book, "Streamlining the Process."
5. A full description of this example is provided in Joann Nagy et al., "Madison: How TQM Helped Change an Admissions Process," *Change* 25, no. 3 (May–June, 1993): 36–40.

LESSON 7

"Measurement without feedback is just data; feedback without measurement is just opinion."

1. One of the best explanations of the PDCA cycle (also known as the Shewhart cycle or the Deming wheel) can be found in Masaaki Imai, *Kaizen: The Key to Japan's Competitive Success* (New York: Random House, 1986), 60–65. In higher education, see Daniel Seymour, *On Q: Causing Quality in Higher Education* (Phoenix, AZ: Oryx Press, 1992), 77–78. A classroom illustration is offered by W. Lee Hansen, "Bringing Total Quality Improvement into the College Classroom," in *CQI 101: A First Reader for Higher Education* (Washington, DC: American Association for Higher Education, 1994), 259.
2. There are many good sources for additional information on performance measurement. For example, see Scott D. Sink and Thomas C. Tuttle, *Planning and*

Measurement in Your Organization of the Future (Norcross, GA: Institute of Industrial Engineers and Management Press, 1989). Also, see Steven M. Hronec, *Vital Signs: Using Quality, Time, and Cost Performance Measurements to Chart Your Company's Future* (New York: American Management Association, 1993).

3. The relationship between measurement and feedback is well explained in two books: H. James Harrington, *Business Process Improvement* (New York: McGraw-Hill, 1991), 164–201; and Eugene H. Melan, *Process Management: Methods for Improving Products and Services* (New York: McGraw-Hill, 1993), 136–38.
4. K. Patricia Cross, "Involving Faculty in TQM," *Community College Journal* 12 (February–March 1993): 16. Also, see Thomas A. Angelo and K. Patricia Cross, *Classroom Assessment Techniques: A Handbook for College Teachers*, 2nd ed. (San Francisco, CA: Jossey-Bass, 1993).
5. John B. Bennett and Elizabeth A. Dreyer, "On Complaining about Students," *AAHE Bulletin* 46, no. 8 (April 1994): 7.

LESSON 8

"Followers, not leaders, are the best judges of hypocrisy."

1. Joel Barker, *Future Edge* (New York: William Morrow, 1992), 163.
2. Steven R. Covey, *Principle-Centered Leadership* (New York: Summit Books, 1990), 62–64.
3. Ibid., 63.
4. Harry I. Forsha, *The Pursuit of Quality through Personal Change* (Milwaukee, WI: ASQC Quality Press, 1992), 3.

LESSON 9

"To create the future, challenge the past."

1. *An American Imperative: Higher Expectations for Higher Education* (Racine, WI: The Johnson Foundation, 1993).
2. Thomas S. Kuhn, *The Structure of Scientific Revolutions* (Chicago: University of Chicago Press, 1970).
3. Ikujiro Nonaka, "The Knowledge-Creating Company," *Harvard Business Review* 69, no. 6 (November–December 1991): 103.
4. Eliyahu M. Goldratt, *The Goal* (Croton-on-Hudson, NY: North River Press, 1992), 31.
5. For many involved in the study of learning organizations—organizations skilled at creating, acquiring, and transferring knowledge, and at modifying their behavior to reflect new knowledge and insights—*dialogue* has become a central element in various models of transformation. A series of articles on the subject can be found in *Organizational Dynamics* 22, no. 2 (Autumn 1993).

6. Chris Argyris and Donald Schon, *Organizational Learning: A Theory of Action Perspective* (Reading, MA: Addison-Wesley, 1978). See also, Chris Argyris, "Teaching Smart People How to Learn," *Harvard Business Review* 69, no. 3 (May–June 1991): 99–109.

LESSON 10

"Exceptional solutions to universal problems create universal problems."

1. W. Edwards Deming devotes a 60-page chapter in *Out of the Crisis* (Cambridge, MA: Massachusetts Institute of Technology Center for Advanced Engineering Study, 1992) to common and special causes of variation. It is worthy of careful study.
2. The term *theory of bad apples* was coined by Donald M. Berwick. A more detailed discussion of the theory is available in his article "Continuous Improvement as an Ideal in Health Care," *The New England Journal of Medicine* 320, no. 1 (January 5, 1989): 53.
3. The practice of benchmarking and searching for best practices is well established in industry. See, for example, Robert C. Camp, *Benchmarking: The Search for Industry Best Practices That Lead to Superior Performance* (Milwaukee, WI: ASQC Quality Press, 1989). There has been some recent interest in the topic in higher education. See Barbara S. Shafer and L. Edwin Coate, "Benchmarking in Higher Education," *Business Office* 26, no. 5 (November 1992): 28–35.

LESSON 11

"Universal solutions to exceptional problems create universal problems."

1. W. Edwards Deming, *Out of the Crisis* (Cambridge, MA: Massachusetts Institute of Technology Center for Advanced Engineering Study, 1982).
2. Walter A. Shewart, a statistician for Bell Laboratories and mentor of W. Edwards Deming, developed process control charts in the 1930s. His book *Statistical Method: From the Viewpoint of Quality Control* (Mineola, NY: Dover Publications, 1986), is the definitive work. A simplified explanation and tips for constructing control charts can be found in George D. Robson, *Continuous Process Improvement* (New York: The Free Press, 1991). Stanley Spanbauer, a former college president, offers a short description of variation, control charts, and a number of education examples in his book *A Quality System for Education* (Milwaukee, WI: American Society for Quality Control, 1992).
3. Robert Cornesky and Samuel McCool, *Total Quality Improvement Guide for Institutions of Higher Education* (Madison, WI: Magna Publications, 1992), 51–76.
4. Adapted from Ellen Earle Chaffee and Lawrence A. Sherr, *Quality: Transforming Postsecondary Education*, ASHE-ERIC Higher Education Report, no. 3 (Washington, DC: The George Washington University, 1992), 52.

5. Pam Walter, "When Is a Problem Not a Problem?" in Deborah J. Teeter and G. Gregory Lozier, *Pursuit of Quality in Higher Education: Case Studies in Total Quality Management,* New Directions for Institutional Research no. 78 (San Francisco: Jossey-Bass, 1993), 111.
6. Deming, 327.

LESSON 12

"Know less, understand more."

1. This chapter is adapted, with permission, from the chapter "Why, Jimmy, Why?" by Maury Cotter and Daniel Seymour, *Kidgets and Other Insightful Stories about Quality in Education* (Milwaukee, WI: American Society for Quality Control, 1993).
2. Daniel H. Kim, "The Link between Individual and Organizational Learning," *Sloan Management Review* (Fall 1993): 37–49.
3. Chris Argyris, *On Organizational Learning* (Cambridge, MA: Blackwell Publishing, 1992). See also, Chris Argyris, *Overcoming Organizational Defenses* (New York: Prentice-Hall, 1990).
4. Donald M. Berwick, A. Blanton Godfrey, and Jane Roessner, *Curing Health Care: New Strategies for Quality Improvement* (San Francisco: Jossey-Bass, 1990).

LESSON 13

"Things do not exist independent of their relationship to other things."

1. Margaret J. Wheatley, *Leadership and the New Science: Learning about Organization from an Orderly Universe* (San Francisco: Berrett-Koehler Publishers, 1992).
2. Ibid., 27.
3. Peter Senge, *The Fifth Discipline* (New York: Doubleday, 1990).
4. The issue of compensating for an undesirable result has been explored through the use of experiments and simulations. The series of Monte Carlo experiments with a funnel that W. Edwards Deming describes in *Out of the Crisis* (Cambridge, MA: Massachusetts Institute of Technology Center for Advanced Engineering Study, 1982), pages 327–32, illustrates the disastrous effects of tampering with a stable process instead of making improvements through fundamental change. Peter Senge illustrates the same phenomenon in his beer game simulation described in chapter 3 of *The Fifth Discipline*. Finally, Maury Cotter, the director of the Office of Quality at the University of Wisconsin—Madison, has developed and uses a higher education simulation that illustrates many of the problems (e.g., unintended consequences, overcompensation) of nonsystemic thinking.
5. Wheatley, 38.
6. A more detailed description of the systems approach taken by Jackson Community College is available in Leslee M. Brockett and Clyde E. LeTarte, "Sys-

tems Thinking," in *Continuous Quality Improvement: Making the Transition to Education* edited by Dean L. Hubbard (Maryville, MO: Prescott Publishing, 1993).

7. The University of Tampa has produced a small booklet, *Quality Process Management for the University of Tampa,* that details its efforts to become "a liberal arts university for a new millennium." Contact the Office of the President, The University of Tampa, 401W. Kennedy Boulevard, Tampa, FL 33606-1490.

8. Peter Senge gives a full explanation of this technique in *The Fifth Discipline,* 73–92.

LESSON 14

"Spread hope."

1. William C. Byham and Jeff Cox, *Zapp! The Lightning Power of Empowerment* (New York: Ballantine Books, 1988).

2. Ibid., 26.

3. Ibid., 54–55.

4. Edward E. Lawler III, *High Involvement Management* (San Francisco, CA: Jossey-Bass, 1986).

5. Ronald W. Clement, "Happy Employees Are Not All Alike," *Across the Board* (January–February 1993): 51–52.

6. A powerful book on extrinsic motivation and why it does not work is Alfie Kohn's *Punished by Rewards* (New York: Houghton Mifflin, 1993). He includes an appendix, "What is intrinsic motivation?"

INDEX

by Janet Perlman

Breinigsville, PA USA
12 April 2011
259715BV00005B/1/P